Practical Strategies for Struggling Learners in
Today's Inclusive Classroom

BY **Ashlea L. Rineer-Hershey**

SLIPPERY ROCK UNIVERSITY

FIRST EDITION

cognella® ACADEMIC PUBLISHING

Bassim Hamadeh, CEO and Publisher
Kassie Graves, Director of Acquisitions and Sales
Jamie Giganti, Senior Managing Editor
Jess Estrella, Senior Graphic Designer
John Remington, Senior Field Acquisitions Editor
Monika Dziamka, Project Editor
Brian Fahey, Licensing Specialist
Christian Berk, Associate Production Editor

Cover image copyright © by Depositphotos/monkeybusiness.

Printed in the United States of America

ISBN: 978-1-5165-1603-2 (pbk) / 978-1-5165-1604-9 (br)

Contents

Preface

This textbook has been designed to be used in college-level undergraduate and graduate courses in the area of elementary, secondary, and special education programs. This text provides a firm background in the need for academic interventions for struggling learners and a plan of action for putting those interventions in place so they are successful in helping students succeed in school.

As I began teaching at Slippery Rock University in the special education department, I was assigned to teach an undergraduate course titled "Interventions in the Content Areas." The course was designed for our undergraduate early childhood and special education students to take in their semester before they entered their student teaching placements. After reviewing the syllabus objectives, I began the search for one textbook that would encompass many of the main topics covered throughout the course. I could not find one. Some texts provided chapters related to a few content areas I needed to cover, but I could not find one textbook that I felt confident requiring my students to purchase.

At that point, I decided I would teach the course using a variety of supplemental materials. After three years teaching the course, I developed a variety of content and activities that I felt strongly fit the need of the course objectives. When Cognella Publishing approached me about writing a textbook for this course, I felt like they read my mind. I hoped that the textbook would be a win for my students as well as other instructors looking for a text like this one.

I sincerely hope that you will find the chapters in this text well written and organized to provide current and future educators the necessary tools and knowledge to provide interventions to assist all of their students in meeting grade-level standards. Each chapter is based in research and effective methodology for working with struggling learners in key areas.

Happy reading!

Acknowledgments

This textbook was developed from a variety of experiences and knowledge gained through the various teaching opportunities I have had over the past fourteen years. Thank you to the incredible teachers I worked with in my first teaching position in the Lampeter-Strasburg School District, as well as the consultants at the Pennsylvania Technical Training and Assistance Network and the members of the department of special education at Slippery Rock University for the opportunity to grow as an educator.

Thank you to all the staff at Cognella Publishing for the support and guidance, especially John Remington and Monika Dziamka.

Thank you to my sweet husband, Shawn, and my children, Finn, Gemma, Polly, and Jett, for their support as I spent time away to work on this textbook.

About the Authors

D r. Ashlea Rineer-Hershey began her teaching career as a special education teacher at Martin Meylin Middle School in Lancaster, Pennsylvania. After concluding her public school teaching career, Dr. Rineer-Hershey spent time working in higher education and as an educational consultant. Eventually, she found her home teaching at Slippery Rock University in the special education department. This is where she found her true calling. She now focuses her energy on teaching future teachers effective instructional practices. Dr. Rineer-Hershey sees higher education as the most effective way she can reach students in the K–12 classroom. She works to impact those students' future teachers by preparing them to be effective educators.

Dr. Rineer-Hershey also currently works as a consultant, training teachers and paraeducators on inclusive practices, co-teaching, behavior, autism, and other topics throughout public schools in western Pennsylvania. Dr. Rineer-Hershey presents at various national and international conferences and has multiple publications related to teacher education and addressing the needs of struggling learners in the classroom.

Dr. Rineer-Hershey lives in Pittsburgh, Pennsylvania, with her husband and four children.

Section I

FOUNDATION

Introduction to Academic Interventions

Chapter Objectives

At the conclusion of the chapter, the reader will be able to:
- Define the term academic intervention
- Review the six-step process to providing interventions for struggling learners
- Define various assessments commonly utilized in schools
- Identify the qualities of a research-based intervention
- Define Response to Intervention
- Review various types of intervention schedules

New Terminology

- Academic Intervention
- At-Risk
- Baseline
- Benchmark
- Curriculum-Based

- Formative
- Intervention Schedule
- Research-Based
- Response to Intervention (RTI)
- Standardized
- Universal Screener

Introduction

In the history of the United States, there have traditionally been groups of students that were underserved by their schools because of their race, gender, ethnicity, first language, or socioeconomic background. Although historically, these students have not received the instruction that met their needs, critical legislation and litigation recently have caused the needs of every student to be considered more seriously. It has become critical for schools to help each child to achieve at their fullest potential. As a result, the implementation of interventions to address the needs of struggling learners has become a part of many classrooms across the country.

This textbook is designed to give educators a clear background on interventions that will address the needs of struggling learners in the classroom. This first chapter will focus on interventions and how they are used to address the needs of struggling learners. Additionally, the importance of using only evidence-based interventions in the classroom will be discussed. A six-step process for identifying interventions that match individual student needs will be described. In future chapters, the text will discuss the legal need for interventions, systems of providing interventions, as well as effective interventions that can be used to address the needs of struggling learners in various content areas.

How do you define intervention as it relates to struggling learners in the classroom?

_____

_____

_____

Overview of Interventions

Intervention is a term used to describe an approach to developing and building a student's academic ability. This is most often done through small group or one-on-one instruction. The area of weakness a student experiences is identified, and then a plan for intervention is developed to focus in on that specific area of struggle. The intervention is provided in addition to the regular academic instruction already occurring in the classroom. It does not replace the current instruction, but builds upon the skills that are weak or that the student is struggling to master. The student's progress is monitored regularly through ongoing assessments to determine if the intervention is working to address the student's weakness or area of struggle.

By providing academic interventions for struggling learners as soon as students begin to fall behind, these students are able to get the help they need to get back on track. The term often used to describe these learners is at-risk. These students are at risk of failure, and the implementation of an effective intervention gives them the opportunity to have their learning needs met quickly and effectively before they develop deficits in the grade-level academic curriculum. This chapter will provide teachers a guide in how to address students that exhibit difficulty and develop a plan to intervene to help them find success in the academic areas where they struggle.

In your experience, what are some characteristics of at-risk learners?

_____

_____

_____

The Six-Step Process for Providing Interventions to Struggling Learners

Step 1: Determine Student Need
Step 2: Assess Deficit Skill Areas
Step 3: Identify Appropriate Research-Based Interventions
Step 4: Develop a Schedule to Provide Intervention Time
Step 5: Implement Intervention(s)
Step 6: Monitor Student Progress

STEP 1: DETERMINE STUDENT NEED

The first step in the process of providing interventions for struggling learners is to determine when students are in need. Chapter 3 will further outline how to effectively assess learners to determine their need for academic interventions. Although teachers recognize that learning is a continual process of growth and improvement, some students require more than what the general education classroom instruction provides in order to adequately master grade-level skills.

There are many reasons for teachers to make every effort to intervene quickly and effectively to address the academic areas of struggle. One reason is to enhance the student's development. Research has established that the quicker we can intervene and address student needs, the more likely a student will be able to get back on track with their grade-level peers. If too much time passes before needs are addressed, a student may run the risk of never having the chance to get back on grade level with their mastery of skills in a specific area of need. Additionally, providing interventions early on will not only benefit the student academically, but also socially and emotionally. Students feel a greater sense of enjoyment for learning, which helps their self-worth as a student and as a peer in the classroom setting. Lastly, identifying and providing effective interventions also has an impact on the long-term success of a student. By helping students reach academic milestones regularly without the consistent feeling of struggle and failure in school, we are able to help students make continued progress through graduation and ultimately have the desire to continue to find success through post-secondary education and a career. In turn, society will reap the benefits.

STEP 2: ASSESS DEFICIT SKILL AREAS

Utilizing a variety of assessment data is critical in determining where students are demonstrating a deficit. Many schools are beginning to adopt screening assessment tools that are used schoolwide or throughout the grade level. Other schools are utilizing data from standardized, benchmark, curriculum-based or formative assessments. A list of assessment types with descriptions is included below. Many schools are using a combination of these tools to determine student needs.

No matter which assessment tools are being implemented to determine students' progress and potential areas of need, teachers must be determined to use only data to drive their instruction. Therefore, teachers must become experienced in the administration of assessments and evaluation of assessment results. The data should then be used to guide the planning of instruction that will best meet the needs of the class of students as well as individual students that are struggling to maintain appropriate grade-level progress.

ASSESSMENT GLOSSARY

Baseline Assessment- A formal type of assessment given to each student at the start of a defined period of time to determine their level of achievement prior to new instruction and/or the beginning of an intervention.

Benchmark Assessment- A short, typically informal test given to students at different points through the year to give immediate feedback as to where they stand in meeting academic standards, per that given year.

Curriculum-Based Assessment- A direct assessment of academic skills. Using the curriculum within the school, the teacher directly assesses the student through observation and records their achievement. Data is then used to make instructional decisions.

Formative Assessment- Typically, a low-stakes assessment that is ongoing to monitor student learning during instruction and help teachers improve their teaching and/or drive their instruction immediately or as they plan for the next day's lesson.

Response to Intervention (RTI)- A commonly used system of providing interventions to struggling learners in classrooms across the nation. This system begins with the administering of a benchmark assessment to determine students' baseline achievement. Students are then placed into three tiered levels based on their academic needs and progress throughout the school year.

Standardized Assessment- A large-scale test with a compilation of multiple-choice, true-and-false, and essay questions that is administered to all students regardless of ability level. The test is then graded in a systematic way. The results make it possible to show the performance of an individual student or groups of students.

Universal Screener (as in identifying struggling learners for RTI) - The first step in RTI that identifies struggling learners. Assessments are brief and at grade level and used with all the students in the classroom or grade level.

What assessment tools does your school use to determine student mastery of grade-level skills?

_____

_____

_____

Which assessment types do you have the most and least experience implementing in the classroom?

_____

_____

_____

STEP 3: IDENTIFY APPROPRIATE RESEARCH-BASED INTERVENTIONS

Once assessment data is gathered, the teacher must use that data to make determinations about the student's deficit area. At that point, the teacher can then begin the process of identifying an appropriate intervention to help get the student back on track with their grade-level peers. It is critical that the teacher is identifying the intervention for the given student that matches most closely to their area of weakness. Criteria should be used when making the decision about the use of an intervention in the classroom.

The intervention chosen must be appropriate for the grade level the student is on, the grade level the student is in, as well as the specific skill area of weakness. Once a list of potential interventions that match these requirements is compiled, the teacher must then determine which of those interventions are supported by research as being effective. Research-based interventions are strategies, teaching methodologies, and supports that have been shown through one or more valid research studies to help a student make gains in the area of weakness. This research will demonstrate that the intervention has been tried out in the classroom with positive benefits for the students in a situation similar to that which the teacher identified with a student in their own classroom.

Once all the necessary data and information is gathered to decide which intervention is most appropriate and beneficial to the at-risk student, then a plan must be put into place to begin the implementation of the intervention. It is critical for the teacher to become knowledgeable

Intervention Resource	How to Access?	What Does It Provide?	Evidence of Research-Based Resource
Intervention Central	www.interventioncentral.org	Intervention Central provides educators free resources to help struggling students attain grade-level standards. This tool provides a variety of academic and behavioral intervention ideas that are supported by research.	A nonprofit organization developed by Jim Wright, an experienced educator and consultant in the area of academic and behavioral interventions in public schools across the country.
The Association for Supervision and Curriculum Development	http://www.ascd.org/research-a-topic/response-to-intervention-resources.aspx	The organization provides information on relevant books, articles, videos, experts, and other resources in the area of RTI. The website includes a list of applicable resources when working with students with all levels of intervention needs.	A nonprofit organization with a mission to provide resources to all members of the education community seeking to promote success for all students.
The RTI Action Network	http://www.rtinetwork.org	The RTI Action Network was developed to assist educators in effectively implementing Response to Intervention (RTI) in schools across the country.	A nonprofit organization developed by the National Center for Learning Disabilities. The RTI Action Network is funded by the Cisco Foundation and partners with leaders in the field of RTI.
IRIS Peabody Center	http://iris.peabody.vanderbilt.edu	The IRIS Peabody Center's website provides free training resources through online modules, videos, podcasts, etc. that support teachers seeking appropriate interventions to meet the needs of students in their classrooms.	A nonprofit organization that was developed by Vanderbilt College and supported through funding from the U.S. Department of Education and the Office of Special Education.

Figure 1–1. Online Intervention Tool Chart

with the implementation before setting up a plan to begin using it with the student. When teaching a student using a specific program, methodology, or strategy, it is important that the teacher is skilled in the facilitation of it in the classroom. Becoming knowledgeable in how to use the intervention, time needed, group setting, and materials are all helpful details the teacher must consider before moving to Step 4.

What types of intervention programs have you implemented in your own classroom?

_____

_____

_____

How did you determine these interventions were based in reliable and valid research?

_____

_____

_____

STEP 4: DEVELOP A SCHEDULE TO PROVIDE INTERVENTION TIME

Depending on the discrepancy between students' current performance level and the benchmark level as well as the protocol described for an individual intervention type, administrators and teachers must work together to develop a schedule that allows students to continue on with core, grade-level instruction with the entire class while also participating in additional instructional time to address areas of weakness. This additional time is often called intervention time and is blocked off in grade-level daily schedules.

Many schools across the nation are choosing to implement systematic intervention time within each grade level. In other situations, individual teachers are seeing the need for additional one-on-one or small group interventions within their classroom and developing their own schedule to provide this. We will come back to the scheduling of intervention time during Chapter 4 when we discuss the systematic intervention system called Response to Intervention (RTI).

George Washington Elementary School First Grade Intervention Schedule Group 1: 9:00-9:15 Group 2: 9:15-9:30			
Skill Focus	**Student Names**	**Strategy Plan**	**Responsible Teacher**
Phonemic Awareness- Blending and Isolating Sounds	**Group 1: Mary Thomas Frank** **Group 2: Jessica Tony Annabelle**	**Build and break apart words** • **Picture cards** • **Letter magnets** • **Beginning, ending, and middle sound sorts** • **Dry erase boards and markers**	**Mrs. Barry**
Count to 100 by 1's, 2's, 5's, and 10's	**Group 1: Hailey Max Joey** **Group 2: Olivia Taylor Jackson**	**Rote counting practice with number charts** • **Highlight patterns with each as it is said** • **Flashcards** • **Counting game on iPad**	**Mrs. Lucarino**

Figure 1–2. Sample Grade-Level Intervention Schedule

Does your school have a standard time built into the day for interventions to be implemented with struggling and at-risk students?

_____

_____

_____

If not, is there a time in your classroom's daily schedule that you could devote to intervention time?

_____

_____

_____

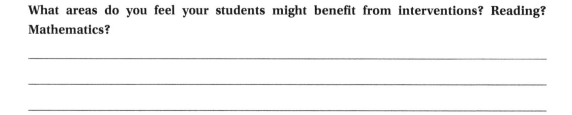

Mrs. Benner's Second Grade Daily Class Schedule	
7:45-8:00	Morning Routine/Morning Work
8:00-8:30	Science/Social Studies
8:30-9:20	Intervention/Enrichment Time
9:20-10:05	Art/Music/PE Rotation
10:05-11:45	Reading/Writing
11:45-12:15	Lunch
12:15-2:00	Math/Math Workstations
2:00-2:15	Recess
2:15-2:45	Reading Workshop/Pack Up
2:45	Dismissal

Figure 1–3. Sample Classroom Intervention Schedule

What areas do you feel your students might benefit from interventions? Reading? Mathematics?

_____

_____

_____

STEP 5: IMPLEMENT INTERVENTION(S)

At this point, the teacher is now ready to begin the implementation of the intervention to the student that is struggling. The teacher will now begin the process of teaching the student consistently with the chosen intervention materials. It is critical that the intervention is implemented consistently based on the schedule developed during Step 4. It is also helpful if the staff working with the student during intervention time remains consistent. If intervention time is missed due to illness or other reasons, this time should be made up, and every effort should be made to keep a regular schedule in place daily or weekly.

STEP 6: MONITOR STUDENT PROGRESS

Most intervention methodologies suggest that data be collected to monitor student progress on a weekly basis. This allows for the teacher to see if a student is responding to the intervention in place. Additionally, it allows for the teacher to make changes more quickly if a student is not responding to the intervention. The research suggests that data be collected regularly and that at least four data points are needed to make a decision about whether the intervention is effective or not.

For example, a reading fluency intervention is put into place with a student for twenty minutes each day. The teacher collects data on the student's reading fluency one time each week; after four weeks have passed, the teacher will have enough information to determine whether the reading fluency intervention is working or not. At that time, the teacher can decide to continue with that intervention or put something else in place.

Conclusion

Chapter 1 has given you an overview of the focus for this text. Developing a plan for providing interventions and then carrying out those interventions through the six-step process was presented in this chapter. Each step was introduced and will be expanded on in greater detail throughout upcoming chapters.

The Six-Step Process for Providing Interventions to Struggling Learners

Step 1: Determine Student Need
Step 2: Assess Deficit Skill Areas
Step 3: Identify Appropriate Research-Based Interventions
Step 4: Develop a Schedule to Provide Intervention Time
Step 5: Implement Intervention(s)
Step 6: Monitor Student Progress

This six-step process will provide teachers with a clear path to follow to assist each of their students to gain academic success. Throughout the upcoming chapters, the steps of the process will be explored in greater detail. Additionally, the author will provide multiple chapters regarding appropriate research-based interventions in various content areas.

Discussion Questions

These questions can be used as a basis for online discussion forums or as a starting point for discussion in the college classroom.

1. Do you currently have an intervention process in place for struggling learners in your school? Do you feel that it supports student needs adequately? Why or why not?

2. What types of intervention schedules have you seen implemented in schools? How much time is devoted to those interventions each school day?

3. Have you been involved in determining what interventions are used in your classroom? If so, how did you make the decision to use a particular type of intervention?

4. Check out the resources listed in Figure 1.1. Choose one source, visit the website, and identify how the information provided from this source could be used in your current or future classroom.

5. Reflect on the intervention schedules in Figures 1.2 and 1.3. Could you see either of these schedules working effectively in your classroom? Why or why not? What supports would need to increase in order to make a schedule like one of these feasible?

CHAPTER 2

Inclusive Education and Its Impact on Today's Classroom

Chapter Objectives

At the conclusion of this chapter, the reader will be able to:
- Identify the key components of inclusive education
- Develop an inclusive vision that addresses the key components
- Analyze historical and legal perspectives

New Terminology

- Individualized Education Program (IEP)
- Individuals with Disabilities Education Improvement Act (IDEIA)
- Individuals with Disabilities Education Act (IDEA)
- Inclusive Education
- Supplementary Aides and Services (SAS)
- Free, Appropriate Public Education (FAPE)

Inclusive Education

Inclusive education or inclusion describes the successful education of students who have special learning needs with the appropriate supports and services to participate and benefit in general classroom settings and other natural environments. Inclusive education implies more than physical proximity between students with and without disabilities. In inclusive schools and classrooms, students with disabilities are valued as contributing members of the school community, leading to a sense of belonging within the classroom and community at large.

Inclusive school buildings and classrooms strive to provide all learners equal access to the general education classroom, general education teacher, and general education peers while still giving these students the individualized programming that meets their needs through special education, English as a Second Language, or other types of support. Additionally, inclusive classrooms allow general education students without a special education diagnosis to receive instruction that addresses their individual strengths, challenges, and diversity.

What does inclusive education mean to you?

How do you define inclusive education?

_____

_____

_____

What does an inclusive school look like to you?

_____

_____

_____

"... the concern is no longer whether to provide inclusive education, but how to implement inclusive education in ways that are both feasible and effective in ensuring schooling success for all children."

—Margaret Mead

An Inclusive Vision

For inclusion to be successful, a school or classroom must adopt an inclusive vision. Within this vision, the building administrator or classroom teacher must instill four critical values into that school or classroom environment.

1. Each student must feel valued.
2. There are high expectations for all students that meet grade-level federal and state standards.
3. Teachers, staff, and administrators must work as a team to meet the needs of all learners.
4. Effective research-based teaching methods must be used at all times in the classroom instruction.

Firstly, all students must be valued as contributing members of their school and classroom. They must feel like their voice matters in the classroom. Teachers must be sure to engage all students in discussion, interaction with peers, and other classroom activities. Each student, no matter what type of emotional, behavioral, social, or academic needs they have, must believe that their teachers and peers respect their thoughts, ideas, and perspectives. Each student must also believe that their teachers believe in the abilities and care of their well-being.

Secondly, an inclusive classroom must be based on high expectations for all students that meet federal and state grade-level standards. Although inclusive classrooms contain students that are at a variety of different ability levels academically, behaviorally, emotionally, and socially, the classrooms must still be rigorous in the instruction planned for the entire classroom. Expectations must be set high for all students, no matter their differences, in order to ensure the highest level of achievement.

Additionally, the teachers, paraprofessionals, other staff members, and administrators must work as a cohesive group to be sure the individual needs of all learners are met. These professionals must collaborate together to develop a plan for students throughout daily lessons, assessments, participation in extracurricular events, and other activities to be sure their educational needs are met. Appropriate accommodations and modifications must be used in order to help each student reach their maximum potential and follow through with the requirements outlined in the Individualized Education Program (IEP).

Lastly, research-based teaching methods must be used at all times in the classroom instruction. It is critical that classroom teachers are implementing only curriculum, strategies, and techniques that are proven by research to be successful and effective for learners with various needs. School administrators must support and guide teachers when they choose new curriculum, programs, and instructional strategies to be implemented in daily instruction.

INCLUSIVE VISION STATEMENT ACTIVITY

A Sample Vision Statement:

"Our district recognizes that each child has unique abilities, talents, and needs. The district is committed to providing, in an accountable partnership with the parents, teachers, staff, and the community, opportunities for each learner to acquire the knowledge, skills, and values to become a responsible, productive citizen."

Based on the Four Requirements for an Inclusive Vision Statement, develop your own for your classroom:

_____

_____

_____

Key Components in Inclusive Schools

In order for a school to maintain an inclusive vision, there are seven key components necessary. Each of these components is critical to creating an environment that welcomes all students into the school building and classroom. Although many schools are attempting to implement increased inclusive practices, the benefits for students is best seen when all components are in place.

1. Leadership
2. School Climate and Structure
3. Student Placement
4. Family and Community Involvement
5. Collaborative Practices
6. Instructional Planning and Practices
7. Supplementary Aids and Services

LEADERSHIP

Within inclusive schools, the school building administrators act as leaders. They work hard to promote a sense of responsibility and shared ownership for each and every student in the school. They provide support to all teachers and staff so they feel they have the necessary means to address the needs of all their students. They then require their teachers to utilize the resources and supports made available to them and follow up regularly to ensure that evidence-based inclusive practices are implemented effectively within every classroom by every teacher in the building.

SCHOOL CLIMATE AND STRUCTURE

All students feel welcomed in an inclusive school. The climate and atmosphere of these schools encourage all students to be contributing members of their school community, to be engaged in activities during the school day as well as participate in extracurricular activities.

Within individual classrooms, the environment is also seen as conducive to meeting individual student challenges and differences. Teachers' roles within the classroom setting are flexible. General education teachers, special education teachers, therapists, paraprofessionals, and other staff work collaboratively. They support each other and build from each other's strengths and expertise to best meet the needs of the diverse learners within each classroom.

Additionally, inclusive schools promote collaborative planning and effective instruction. Teachers and other staff have the opportunity to meet regularly to discuss student needs, co-plan lessons, develop appropriate assessment techniques, prepare IEP goals, and review progress monitoring data. They also have the opportunity to participate in professional development training on research-based instructional strategies that are proven effective with various types of learners.

STUDENT PLACEMENT

When making decisions about the appropriate education placement for special education students, the first consideration is always the general education classroom with the use of supplementary aids and services in inclusive schools. Supplementary aids and services are any accommodations, modifications, or educational services that can be put into place to assist a student within the classroom or other school settings. IEP teams must be sure to address the individual needs of each student and then make a determination about what educational placement can address those needs while allowing the student the greatest opportunity to have access to the general education classroom, curriculum, and typical peers. Each student must be given the opportunity to be a part of the general education classroom with any necessary supplementary aids and services put in place to help them find success.

In inclusive schools, all general educators expect to have students with the full range of disabilities in their classrooms for meaningful portions of the day. As a result, these teachers are knowledgeable in the available supplementary aids and services that can be helpful to these students and put these in place when needed. Additionally, these teachers make sure all students are welcome members of the classroom. They also utilize the IEP team to help make the most appropriate decisions for how to help students to be successful in their educational placement. The team reflects collaboratively on what they know about the student, their needs and challenges, and the curriculum and classroom demands. They then identify the skills, settings, and/or activities where the student will need assistance to be successful. A helpful list of the roles and responsibilities of the various members of the IEP team are included below.

FAMILY AND COMMUNITY INVOLVEMENT

Within inclusive schools, families are collaborative partners in all activities. They are invited to be members of community and school organizations. They are encouraged to share information and develop relationships with other families and school staff. Families are seen as critical partners in education, just as important as teachers and the students themselves. Inclusive schools make sure families feel valued and encouraged by school administrators, teachers, and staff. Families are given the opportunity to get actively involved in their child's education.

COLLABORATIVE PRACTICES

Educators collaborate to minimize curricular barriers for special education students included within the general education classroom. By evaluating a student's Individualized Education Program (IEP), collaborative teams identify linkages between IEP goals and content standards to provide access to the general curriculum. This allows a student to learn grade-level material with the appropriate modification and accommodations identified based on their specific needs.

Collaborative teams in inclusive schools also focus on instructional planning and problem solving. Units and lesson plans are developed to maintain the attention and interest of all learners while addressing all instructional levels within one classroom. The instruction is designed specifically to meet the needs of various learners and to be adjusted when a student concern arises. The emotional, behavioral, social, and academic challenges of every student are taken into consideration in these classrooms.

ROLE	RESPONSIBILITIES
IEP Case Manager/ Special Education Teacher	• Facilitates the meeting • Shares expertise and knowledge of how a student's disability impacts the way they access information, learn key concepts, and demonstrate their learning • Provides current information, research, student assessment, and progress reporting data to guide the team in making IEP decisions • Helps general educators adapt their teaching techniques and individualize or modify the curriculum to create classroom goals, flexible methods, materials, and assessments to meet the challenge of learner variability • Assists the team in finding ways to include the student in all aspects of the regular school program, including extra-curricular activities
Local Education Agency (LEA) Representative/ School District Administrator	• Helps to facilitate the meeting • Makes sure team members are given the opportunity to participate as full members of the team • Provides information about the services available in the school • Ensures that services in the IEP will be provided as agreed upon by the team
General Educator	• Shares expertise and knowledge of curriculum and content • Communicates what the student should be able to know and do in order to demonstrate key concepts • Provides information about the student's participation, performance, progress, and interactions with peers in the classroom • Identifies training, materials, or other classroom supports teachers may need in order to help the student benefit from classroom instruction • Identifies areas of concern and determines appropriate instructional and behavioral intervention and supports and other strategies for the student to be meaningfully included in the classroom
Service Providers— Occupational Therapist, Speech-Language Pathologist, Behavior Specialist, etc.	• Shares expertise and knowledge of how a student's disability impacts the way they learn in the specific areas of focus for each therapist/specialist. • Provides current information, research, student assessment, and progress reporting data to guide the team in making IEP decisions specific to their therapy or service • Helps general educators adapt their teaching techniques and individualize or modify classroom activities that will support the student specific to their therapy or service • Locates alternate teaching materials, assistive technology devices, and other needed resources related to their therapy or service
Parent	• Provides critical information about their child's abilities, interests, preferences, and history • Shares information about what has worked for their child over time • Participates in the discussion about their child's need for special education services, activities, and supports • Knows the child better than any other member of the team

Figure 2–1. IEP Team Member Roles and Responsibilities

INSTRUCTIONAL PLANNING AND PRACTICES

Effective instruction within inclusive classrooms incorporates a variety of instructional practices to try to meet varied student needs. Multilevel instruction, active engagement techniques, various methods of assessment, modified assignments, and technology are all implemented to be sure all student needs are met. IEP teams will also identify and teach skills needed to access, participate, and progress in general education curriculum in inclusive schools. Additionally, they will then coordinate and plan services outside the general education classroom to maximize learning in the general education classroom. For example, students may receive social skills instruction with a guidance counselor or additional speech therapy in an individualized setting with a speech and language pathologist. These services are put into place for a student so they can be more successful while in the general education classroom with their typical peers.

SUPPLEMENTARY AIDS AND SERVICES (SAS)

Inclusive schools and classrooms provide a systematic and individualized approach to identification of supports and services for students with disabilities in general education classrooms. Any supports—from simplistic items like pencil grippers for students with fine motor skill deficits to highly technical communication devices for a student with autism who is nonverbal—can be identified to support a student's inclusion in the general education classroom.

SAS is often broken up into five broad categories of supports: Instructional, Environmental, Social and Behavioral, School Personnel/Parental, and Program Modifications. Some examples are provided below under each category. However, this list is just a start, and an IEP team can choose to design individualized supports that help the students to be successful.

Additionally, IEP teams will work to make sure that related services and other supports are delivered in the general education classroom when possible so that special education students have a greater opportunity to be part of the general education classroom with their typical peers. Speech therapy, physical therapy, occupational therapy, and counseling services can all be made available to students within the general education classroom. Specialists and general educators can collaborate to develop, implement, monitor, and adjust positive behavioral supports for students' challenging behaviors within the school community as well.

Category	Examples
School Personnel/ Parental Support Supports/Training for personnel and parents to provide services and to promote adults working together to support students	• Scheduled time for co-planning and team meetings • Instructional arrangements that support collaboration • Coaching and guided support for team members in the use of assistive technology for an individual student • Scheduled opportunities for parental collaboration • Coordination of support services for crisis prevention and intervention • Extracurricular/non-academic providers support • Occupational therapist consult
Instructional Support Development and delivery of instruction that addresses diverse learning needs	• Provide alternate ways for students to demonstrate learning • Provide alternate materials and/or assistive technology (e.g., materials on tape, transcribe text in Braille, large print, alternate computer access) • Provide instruction on functional skills in the context of the typical routines in the regular classroom • Change method of presentation • Provide instructional adaptations (e.g., pre-teaching, repeating directions, extra examples and non-examples) • Provide assistance with organization • Provide home sets of textbooks and materials • Provide proofreading checklist • Provide student with copy of student/teacher notes
Physical Support Adaptations and modifications to the physical environment	• Furniture arrangement in environments • Specific seating arrangements • Individualized desk, chair, etc. • Adaptive equipment • Adjustments to sensory input (e.g., light, sound) • Environmental aids (e.g., classroom acoustics, heating, ventilation) • Structural aids (e.g., wheelchair accessibility, trays, grab bars)
Social-Behavioral Supports and services to increase appropriate behavior and developing relationships with peers	• Social skills instruction • Counseling supports • Peer supports (e.g., facilitating friendships) • Individualized behavior support plans • Modification of rules and expectations • Cooperative learning strategies • Home-school communication system
Program Modifications Adaptations to the content and structure of curriculum and assessments to make them more accessible to the student	• Modified content • Modified grading system • Open-book exams • Reduce number of answer choices • Reduce length of exams • Revise format of tests (fewer questions, fill-in-the-blank) • Delete extraneous information on assignments and assessments • Limit amount of required reading

Figure 2-2. Supplementary Aids and Services Category Guide

In some cases, supports that are identified for students on their IEPs are supports that a teacher may already be planning to provide for the entire class. For example, when the teacher gives a writing assignment, they may give the entire class access to graphic organizers and a computer (word processor) to complete the assignment. These are supports already built into the lesson and will benefit all students. When planning any lesson, these overall strategies and supports should be identified, as well as additional supports that may be needed to eliminate barriers that some students with IEPs may still encounter.

Some helpful tools to keep teachers organized when planning instruction to meet the needs of a variety of learners are provided below. The Supplementary Aids and Services Matrix provides a visual graphic organizer that shows common SAS that may be identified for students within a classroom. The matrix provides teachers with a one-page visual

Supplementary Aids and Services Matrix														
Student Name	graphic/organizational aids	allow use of manipulatives	check for understanding	frequent and immediate feedback	have student paraphrase information	peer buddy or partner work	alternative ways to demonstrate learning	spell checker	word processor	copy of student/teacher notes	reminders to stay on task	word banks	chunking of text	oral exams	behavior contract
Lydia Samson	X		X					X	X	X					
Sarah Wilson	X	X	X	X		X		X	X	X	X	X			
Timothy Ryan	X	X	X	X	X	X	X		X	X	X	X	X	X	X

Figure 2–3. SAS Matrix

Supplementary Aids and Services WHEN Guide		
When:	**Students are expected to:**	**We will provide these supports:**
The teacher is talking	Remain seated at desks Orient toward front of the room Look at board Take notes	Seat near front (Sam, Tyler) Seat near back (Rebecca) Own copy of slides/overhead (Julie) Cloze notes (Alex, Sam, Tyler)
Teacher guides whole class discussion	Remain seated Remain quiet when others are speaking Raise hand to be acknowledged Answer questions Contribute to discussion	Visual cue for hand raising (Julie) Preplanned question to answer (Tyler) Behavioral feedback (Julie)
Cooperative group or pair activities	Take turns Complete assigned role/task Interact politely with peers	Assigned role that doesn't require writing (Julie, Tyler) Written copy of the directions (Rebecca, Alex) Behavioral feedback (Sam)
Teacher-directed small groups/guided reading	Participate actively during group Work quietly and independently on anchor activities when not in group Ask peers for assistance if needed when not in group	Task schedule and timer for independent time (Rebecca) "3-before-me" visual reminder (Rebecca, Alex) Anchor activities at independent/practice level of difficulty (all students)
Individual seatwork	Remain seated and quiet Complete written task Ask for help if needed	Reduced writing requirement and/or scribe (Alex, Liam) Chunking (Alex, Rebecca, Julie) Reduced complexity (Alex) Breaks (Rebecca)

Figure 2–4. SAS When Guide

that displays the necessary SAS needed for each student. If you require more detail to outline the SAS needs of each student in your classroom when particular expectations are in place for students, the Supplementary Aids and Services When Guide provides a detailed list of SAS that will be provided to students during different events of the day. Blank versions of these templates are provided in the Resources section at the end of the text.

Federal Legislation

An Exclusionary Past: Children who are different have often been denied full and fair access to educational opportunities. Throughout history, various groups of children for various reasons have been denied access to a quality education. Various minority groups, children with disabilities, children speaking other languages, and children from low-income areas have all been denied access to a quality education. For this reason, federal legislation had to be put in place to protect the rights of every child in the United States.

Separate Is Not Equal: Special education was strongly influenced by the social developments and court decisions that occurred in the 1950s and 1960s (e.g., *Brown v. Board of Education*). As a result, legislation was put into place to ensure the protection of these children and to ensure that they would be entitled to the same quality education as any other child in the United States. Equal protection is critical to be sure that all children are entitled to a free, appropriate public education no matter their race, ethnicity, socioeconomic background, gender, or disability.

THE LEGISLATION THAT MANDATES INCLUSIVE EDUCATION

The Individuals with Disabilities Education Improvement Act (IDEIA) has been the most influential piece of legislation specific to school-age children with disabilities. This federal law is quite extensive and has been influential in creating the Individualized Education Program (IEP) and developing an evaluation process for first identifying special education students. Additionally, it outlines critical components of special education that must be made available to every student that qualifies for an IEP within the United States.

The year 1975 was the very start of IDEA. Legislation was introduced and titled the Education of All Handicapped Children Act. In 1990, the "Education of All Handicapped Children Act" was renamed "Individuals with Disabilities Education Act." Years later in 1997, several important amendments were made to the legislation as well. The most recent amendment was made in 2004, when the addition of development disability was added to the types of disability categories as well as provided a clear process for parents and schools to resolve disputes. The most recent revision to this federal law was in 2004, when IDEA was amended by the Individuals with Disabilities Education Improvement Act (IDEIA). Several new additions were made that aligned more closely to the No Child Left Behind Act of 2001.

The Major Purposes of IDEA:

1. To ensure that all children have available to them a free, appropriate public education (FAPE)
2. To ensure that the rights of children with disabilities and their parents are protected
3. To assist state and local educational agencies in providing for the education of children with disabilities
4. To ensure the necessary tools are available to improve educational results for children with disabilities
5. To assess and ensure the effectiveness of efforts to educate children with disabilities

The Individuals with Disabilities Education Act (IDEA) is the piece of legislation that has had the most impact on inclusive education in the history of education in the United States. IDEA has provided a foundation to regulate the provision of special education services to students across our country. It provides schools with the mandates necessary to give each child the services they require to help them be successful in the classroom based on their individual learning needs.

ADDITIONAL RELATED LEGISLATION

In addition to IDEA, there is other legislation that has been critical in the development of special education and the importance of inclusive education in today's schools and classrooms. These laws, along with IDEA, have shaped the United States' educational system and allow this country to provide the opportunity for general and special education students to be educated together while still allowing each child's individual needs to be met.

AMERICANS WITH DISABILITIES ACT

The Americans with Disabilities Act (ADA) extends civil rights protection to private sector employment, all public services, public accommodations, and transportation. It was signed into law on July 26, 1990, and then in 2008, the ADA Amendments Act (ADAAA) was passed. The ADA provides protection for individuals with disabilities outside of their time in schools and classrooms. It allows people of all ages with all types of disabilities to gain access to and be a part of events, activities, and employment in many locations and business types. With the protection of ADA, all individuals can utilize public bus systems, the U.S. railroad, and facilities like restaurants, hotels, and grocery stores, and they cannot be discriminated against because of a disability when seeking employment.

ELEMENTARY AND SECONDARY EDUCATION ACT
(A.K.A. NO CHILD LEFT BEHIND ACT)

The Elementary and Secondary Education Act (ESEA) was first signed into law in 1965 by President Lyndon Johnson, who believed that "full educational opportunity" should be "our first national goal." This legislation offered grants to schools that served low-income students as well as funding to improve library and text resources. Additionally, the law issued federal grant money to states to improve the quality of education at the elementary and secondary levels.

Congress reauthorized ESEA and President George W. Bush signed the law in 2002, giving it a new name, No Child Left Behind (NCLB). The intent of NCLB is to improve the achievement of all students, with a particular emphasis on children from low-income families. States were expected to make annual progress toward the 100% proficiency goal by 2014, which was obviously unachievable. NCLB puts a special emphasis on using educational programs and practices that rigorous scientific research has demonstrated to be effective. The provisions of NCLB apply to all students, including those with disabilities. While NCLB put in place measures that exposed achievement gaps among traditionally underserved students and started an important discussion on the need for educational improvement in the United States, the law is long overdue for reauthorization.

Many parents, educators, and elected officials have recognized that a strong, updated law is necessary to expand opportunity for students, schools, and teachers in the U.S. In 2012, the Obama administration began offering flexibility to states regarding the requirements of NCLB in exchange for state plans that are designed to close achievement gaps among traditionally underserved students, improve the quality of instruction, and increase academic achievement for all students. So far, forty-two states, Washington, D.C., and Puerto Rico have received flexibility from NCLB.

Conclusion

This chapter addressed the importance of inclusive education in order to best meet the needs of special education students. Critical components of successful inclusion in schools and classrooms are Leadership, School Climate and Structure, Student Placement, Family and Community Involvement, Collaborative Practices, Instructional Planning and Practices, and Supplementary Aids and Services. With the combination of these, schools are able to adhere to the requirements of IDEA and other legislation. Providing all students with the opportunity to be included in all aspects of the regular school day gives general and special education students the chance to have access to the general education setting, general education curriculum, and typical peers.

By following through with the guidelines of IDEA and other legislation, it is critical that we meet the needs of all students any way possible. The use of interventions within the general education classroom and sometimes in separate settings is critical. The remaining chapters will discuss the need for effective implementation of evidence-based interventions to help students find success in the classroom. Chapter 3 will continue with a step-by-step plan for how to identify student needs, and the following chapters will address how to carry out that plan. Every student that enters your classroom deserves the opportunity and support necessary to find success.

Discussion Questions

These questions can be used as a basis for online discussion forums or as a starting point for discussion in the college classroom.

1. Find out what the vision is for your school or school district. Does this vision statement meet the guidelines from this chapter? How could you improve this vision statement to contain a clearer focus on inclusion?

2. Is there any litigation from your state that has impacted the use of inclusive practices in schools in your area? What was the reason for these court cases? How did the final decision in these court cases influence inclusive practices in your area?

3. There was a great deal of negative attention given to the No Child Left Behind Act of 2002. Do you see any positives that have come out of the implementation of NCLB for children with disabilities educated in public schools across the United States?

4. What Supplementary Aids and Services (SAS) do you utilize in your classroom to support students with disabilities?

5. Which category of Supplementary Aids and Services from the five broad categories of supports—Instructional, Environmental, Social and Behavioral, School Personnel/ Parental, and Program Modifications—do you utilize most to support your students?

Why? Which do you utilize the least? Why do you feel this is, and how could you make sure your students are better supported in this area in the future?

Chapter Activity

1. Read the article entitled "Inclusion and the Other Kids: Here's What Research Shows so Far About Inclusion's Effect on Nondisabled Students" by Deb Staub (1996). Respond to the questions when you are finished reading the article.

GUIDED QUESTIONS

1. Will the nondisabled students suffer because of inclusion?

2. Will the nondisabled students receive less attention from their teacher?

3. What does the research say about nondisabled students and ...
   - Friendships?
   - Social skills?
   - Self-esteem?
   - Personal principles?
   - Comfort level with people who are different?
   - Patience?

Section II

THE PLAN FOR PROVIDING APPROPRIATE AND QUALITY INTERVENTIONS

CHAPTER 3

Identification and Assessment of Student Learning Needs

Chapter Objectives

At the conclusion of this chapter, the reader will be able to:
- Identify the six-step process for providing interventions
- Define the purpose of a benchmark assessment
- Identify four purposes of a benchmark assessment
- Determine an appropriate benchmark assessment tool for use in your school or classroom
- Determine how to use a benchmark assessment as a screener to identify at-risk students

New Terminology

- State Standardized Assessment
- Early Intervention

Introduction

This chapter is focused on Step 1 and Step 2 of the intervention process introduced in Chapter 1. The two steps are focused on determining student needs and assessing deficit skill areas. The use of benchmark assessments will be presented as a foundation in the process of determining which students in the classroom are in need of potential interventions and what deficits they may exhibit. The purposes for using benchmark assessments are explored as well. Additionally, this chapter explores various benchmark assessment tools developed by reputable companies to evaluate student achievement and monitor progress.

This chapter also explores various scenarios that require the reader to apply their new knowledge from the chapter to determine student needs. The scenarios and questions posed throughout the chapter allow the reader to apply the chapter topics to real-world situations in today's classrooms.

The Six-Step Process for Providing Interventions to Struggling Learners

Step 1: Determine Student Need
Step 2: Assess Deficit Skill Areas
Step 3: Identify Appropriate Research-Based Interventions
Step 4: Develop a Schedule to Provide Intervention Time
Step 5: Implement Intervention(s)
Step 6: Monitor Student Progress

Step 1: Determine Student Need

The first step in the process of providing interventions for struggling learners is to determine when students are in need. Although many teachers understand that learning is a continual process of growth and improvement, some students require more than what the general education classroom instruction typically provides in order to adequately make that necessary growth. Teachers can often feel overwhelmed in a full classroom of students with varying learning needs. When their instruction is not effective with some students, they may feel frustrated and unsure of what to do next.

As classroom teachers, it is critical that we take responsibility for the learning of all students in our classroom. Special education, at-risk, gifted, and the English as a Second Language learners are all entitled to membership in the general education classroom with the supports necessary to help them be successful. The most effective way to determine our students' learning needs is to make an initial assessment of where they are with their academic progress. According to the research in the area of assessment, a benchmark assessment tool should be administered to all students at the beginning of the school year in the major content areas of English/Language Arts and Mathematics.

Benchmark Assessments

Benchmark assessments are designed to give students, teachers, administrators, and parents critical information about students' achievement. If used correctly, benchmark assessment data can be integral in designing classroom instruction that effectively meets the needs of all learners. Benchmark assessments serve multiple purposes in the classroom setting.

PURPOSES OF A BENCHMARK ASSESSMENT

1. Give expectations for student learning: Benchmark assessments are designed to align with federal and state standards and give educators a clear idea of what students are expected to learn in a given content area and grade level. This purpose is helpful in allowing teachers to clearly see how students will be evaluated and make sure their instruction addresses those skill areas.

2. Help teachers to plan effective instruction: These assessments clearly outline what skills students need to master in order to be scored successfully. This allows teachers to then design effective instruction that addresses those skill areas. They can utilize creative instructional strategies that help students master the necessary skills.

3. Evaluate students' learning throughout the school year: Benchmark assessments are designed to be given at least three to five times per year. Because of this, teachers are given constant data showing students' progress or lack of progress. This allows teachers to more quickly intervene and address the needs of a student who is struggling so they can get back on track before too much time passes.

4. Predict how students will perform in the future: One final purpose for benchmark assessments is to predict how students will perform on future assessments—in particular, their performance on state standardized testing. This allows schools to have a constant gauge on

how students are progressing and what they can expect for student performance on yearly state assessments. School administrators and teachers can then plan to make changes to instructional time, intervention needs, etc. so that their school or classroom of students have a better opportunity for success on those state assessments.

(Adapted from Datause.cse.ucla.edu)

Can you come up with any other reasons why students, teachers, administrators, or parents might see a benefit to using benchmark assessments?

_____

_____

_____

HOW TO UTILIZE BENCHMARK ASSESSMENT DATA

By utilizing the benchmark assessment at the start of the school year, also called a benchmark screener, teachers are able to get a baseline score for where each student is prior to beginning their instruction. A baseline score gives teachers an idea of what skills a student has mastered already and where they are in need of additional instruction. Teachers can use this data to look at the class, as a whole, as well as individual students. If particular students perform poorly on the benchmark screener, the teachers can flag these students as at-risk and begin to keep a close eye on their progress and then determine a plan for intervention with them. For the entire class, teachers can then begin their instruction and plan for the benchmark assessment to be re-administered throughout the remainder of the school year.

HOW OFTEN ARE BENCHMARK ASSESSMENTS ADMINISTERED?

Research supports the use of a benchmark assessment three to five times during the year in addition to the first administration to get a baseline score for each student (National Center for Learning Disabilities, 2017). This provides teachers with constant data every two to three months during the school year to monitor student progress. Teachers are able to then see how the students are progressing overall. This gives them the opportunity to reflect on whether their classroom instruction is effective. Additionally, it allows teachers to look specifically at individual students to determine if an intervention that may have been put into place after the previous benchmark assessment results were analyzed had a positive impact on the student's progress. Lastly, the new data allows teachers to determine if there are any new students of concern that don't seem to be making adequate progress. These students may require an intervention to be put into place to help them be more successful and get back on track with their own academic gains.

How to identify the most appropriate benchmark assessment for your school or classroom:
1. Is the assessment aligned to your state standards?
2. Does the publisher utilize an online report tool?
3. Does the publisher provide support and training?
4. What content areas does the assessment evaluate?
5. What is the cost of this assessment versus others?
6. Ask for sample materials to try out.

Many developers of benchmark assessments are gearing their assessment tools to meet the needs of classroom teachers in various states across the country. It is important when searching for an assessment that meets your needs to find one that is aligned to your state standards and is available in the various content areas you are requiring. Also, look for an assessment developer that provides support and training for school staff. It is also important that there be an online report tool where teachers can log in and see students' results and utilize online graphing tools to track class and individual student progress. Additionally, the cost of the assessment is important to consider. There are many companies out there competing for a school's business. It is important to research and compare costs to determine the best option for your school. When you've gathered this critical information, also ask for samples that can be implemented in the classroom and then reflect on their ease of use, etc. By considering all of these factors, your school will have an excellent chance of identifying a benchmark assessment that will best meet its needs and provide helpful information in supporting all students to find success in the classroom.

Does your district utilize a benchmark assessment? What is the name of the assessment?

_____

_____

_____

Assessment Name	Recommended Testing Schedule	Content Areas	Grade Levels	Helpful Tips
4Sight Benchmark Assessment Author: Success for All Foundation	5 times per school year 1 Baseline Assessment Quarterly Assessments	Reading Mathematics	Grades 3–8	Online data management system available. Free samples available from company. Can be developed to align with a specific state's core standards.
Fountas & Pinnell Benchmark Assessment System (BAS) Author: Fountas & Pannell	4 times per year 1 Baseline Assessment 3 Trimester Assessments	Reading	Grades K–8	Online data management system available. Free samples available from company.
DIBELS DIBELS Next Author: University of Oregon	4 times per year 1 Baseline Assessment 3 Trimester Assessments	Reading	Grades K–6	Online data management system available. Free samples available from company. The DIBELS data system has been in place since 2001.

Figure 3–1. Commonly Used Benchmark Assessments

How often is the benchmark assessment given?

_____

_____

_____

What do you do with this assessment data?

_____

_____

_____

The Six-Step Process for Providing Interventions to Struggling Learners

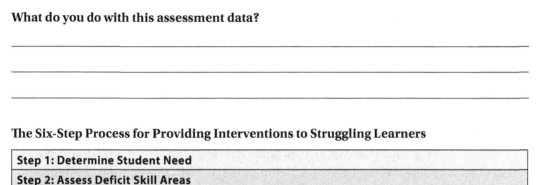

Step 1: Determine Student Need
Step 2: Assess Deficit Skill Areas
Step 3: Identify Appropriate Research-Based Interventions
Step 4: Develop a Schedule to Provide Intervention Time
Step 5: Implement Intervention(s)
Step 6: Monitor Student Progress

Step 2: Assess Deficit Skill Areas

In Step 2 of the intervention process, the teacher needs to assess deficit skill areas in the identified student of concern. The next section will review the use of a benchmark assessment to evaluate all students but to flag the students of concern.

HOW SHOULD BENCHMARK ASSESSMENT DATA BE UTILIZED?

Benchmark data can be used to look at a group of students as a whole or to look at a specific student. The first option allows teachers to use the data results to evaluate the progress their class of students is making. They can compare the current assessment data to the previous data when the last benchmark assessment was given. This allows the teachers to decide if their instruction is helping the students to make progress on the skill areas evaluated.

Additionally, teachers can use the benchmark data to look at individual students. Individual student scores can be reviewed to determine if a student is making continual gains on skill areas as the school year progresses. Students who are not making adequate progress can be flagged for increased monitoring or a plan for intervention can be put into place. The use of benchmark assessment data to review individual student progress is very important. It allows teachers to catch students who are struggling and to intervene early, also known as early intervention.

Scenario:

Mrs. Belkot is a second-grade teacher. During the second week of school, she administered a benchmark assessment to her entire class. The assessment evaluated students in the areas of oral reading fluency. Students were scored based on the number of words read correctly per minute (WCPM). Below is the chart that shows the results for the entire class.

Teacher Name	Average Oral Reading Fluency Score for class	Second-Grade Benchmark (beginning of the school year)
Mrs. Belkot	54 WCPM	52 WCPM

Additionally, Mrs. Belkot received data about each student individually in the classroom. She was able to use this data to compare the student skill level now versus where they should be. Mrs. Belkot was able to use this information to determine if a student needs additional monitoring or if a plan for intervention needs to be developed. Below is the data for one student named Eden.

Student Name	Oral Reading Fluency Score	Second-Grade Benchmark (beginning of the school year)
Eden	36 WCPM	52 WCPM

Check out the additional information regarding benchmark goals for the DIBELS program at https://dibels.uoregon.edu/.../DIBELSNextRecommendedBenchmarkGoals.pdf.

Based on the data provided, how would you continue your instruction for the entire class?

_____

_____

_____

Based on the individual data for Eden, what conclusions would you draw about her progress? How might you provide additional support for this student?

_____

_____

_____

Reasons for Early Intervention

There are many reasons for teachers to make every effort to intervene quickly and effectively to address a student's academic areas of struggle. One reason is to enhance the student's development. Research has established that the quicker we can intervene and address student needs, the more likely a student will be able to get back on track with their grade-level peers (Connor & Morrison, 2014). If too much time passes before needs are addressed, a student may run the risk of never having the chance to get back on grade level with their mastery of skills in a specific area of need.

Additionally, providing interventions early on will not only benefit the student academically, but also socially and emotionally. Students feel a greater sense of enjoyment for learning, which helps their self-worth as a student and as a peer in the classroom setting.

Lastly, identifying and providing effective interventions also has an impact on the long-term success of a student. By helping students reach academic milestones regularly without the consistent feeling of struggle and failure in school, we are able to help students make continued progress through graduation and ultimately have the desire to continue to find success through post-secondary education, employment, and a career.

In your experience, what are some reasons students may require early intervention?

_____

_____

_____

Conclusion

This chapter leads us through the first two steps of the intervention process first introduced in Chapter 1. Step 1, Determine Student Need, was discussed in great detail. The use of benchmark assessments was introduced as a way to identify the at-risk students in a classroom. The author reviewed the definition and purpose of utilizing benchmark assessments. Step 2, Assess Deficit Skill Areas, was also reviewed. Again, the use of benchmark assessments was discussed as a way to determine which areas specific students may need remediation or review to obtain mastery of grade-level skills. The term and importance of early intervention was also discussed in this portion of Chapter 3

Future chapters will lead us through the remaining steps of the intervention process presented in this text.

Discussion Questions

These questions can be used as a basis for online discussion forums or as a starting point for discussion in the college classroom.

1. Evaluate the benchmark assessment used in your school. Do you feel the data from this assessment is used to drive instruction in the classrooms in your school? Why or why not?

2. Choose one of the benchmark assessments described in Figure 3.1 and research it further. Based on the information you learned in Chapter 3 regarding benchmark assessments, do you feel this would be a helpful tool for your own classroom? Why or why not?

3. Summarize Steps 1 and 2 of the intervention process presented in this chapter. Do you follow through with these steps in your classroom? If not, what changes could you make to follow these steps more closely?

4. If a school is not currently utilizing a benchmark assessment to gather data about its students, what steps would you suggest it take before purchasing an assessment tool to be sure it finds the most appropriate one?

Identify Appropriate Research-Based Interventions

Chapter Objectives

At the conclusion of this chapter, the reader will be able to:
- Review Step 3 of the intervention process: Match Appropriate Research-Based Interventions with Student Needs
- Understand how to implement an intervention action plan
- Learn about research-based interventions and strategies for learners struggling in different content areas

New Terminology

- Intervention Action Plan
- Intervention Objective

The Six-Step Process for Providing Interventions to Struggling Learners

Step 1: Determine Student Need
Step 2: Assess Deficit Skill Areas
Step 3: Identify Appropriate Research-Based Interventions
Step 4: Develop a Schedule to Provide Intervention Time
Step 5: Implement Intervention(s)
Step 6: Monitor Student Progress

Introduction

Throughout Chapter 4, important information regarding how to determine what interventions may be appropriate for a student based on their needs will be discussed. A Plan of Action template will be presented as a way to work through the 6-step process to provide appropriate interventions for students. This template will be reviewed along with an example to help readers understand how to implement the action plan in their own classroom. Additionally, the chapter will review various evidence-based interventions and strategies that are effective in various content areas.

The Intervention Action Plan

An Intervention Action Plan is a plan created to organize an educator's effort to work toward improving the skills of a struggling learner. Action plans are developed with a main goal in mind. When considering an action plan focused on intervention, the goal is to take a student's identified deficit areas and match them with appropriate instructional interventions and teaching strategies so that a concrete plan for improving the deficit skills can be determined.

A template that can be utilized to develop Intervention Action Plans with your own students is included at the end of this chapter. This action plan contains six key components.

The Six Components of an Intervention Action Plan
1. Present Academic Level
2. Intervention Objective(s)
3. Action Step
4. Time

5. Materials/Resources
6. Person Responsible

PRESENT ACADEMIC LEVEL

This section provides a space for the teacher to summarize the academic needs of the students in this area. Additionally, this section should include any assessment data that helped the teacher to determine that this was an area of need for the student.

For example,

Mark is struggling with his letter sound recognition. After a baseline assessment was given during the first week of school, he scored only a 0/26 with his letter sound recognition. Based on benchmark data, Mark should be scoring at least 4/26 at letter sound recognition at the beginning of the school year (based on the PALS Reading Program Benchmark Data, 2016). His teacher, Mrs. McKee, is concerned Mark will fall further behind as the year progresses. At the beginning of October, she decides to work with him and two other students with similar baseline scores for a ten-minute intervention block each day.

INTERVENTION OBJECTIVE

This section of the action plan template provides a space for the teacher to develop a very specific objective for the student during the intervention time. The objective must be measurable, clear, and concise so the teacher is able to accurately assess the student's progress in this area.

HOW TO WRITE A CLEAR OBJECTIVE:

CONDITION + BEHAVIOR + DEGREE + EVALUATION

Condition = under which the behavior will be performed
Behavior = exhibited by the student as a result of the lesson
Degree = of accuracy for mastery
Evaluation = of student performance, how will data be collected, form/checklist/worksheet/quiz

It is possible that an action plan may contain more than one objective. Once the objectives from an action plan are met and a student continues to struggle in some way, then additional and more strategic objectives are developed.

Objective Example:

Given a list of letters, Mark will improve his letter-naming fluency to reach the grade-level benchmark of 4/26 for the fall and 17/26 by midyear, as demonstrated on progress monitoring data taken each week.

ACTION STEP

This section of the action plan template outlines the steps that will need to be taken to make sure the intervention time is used effectively to help the student make progress in the deficit skill areas. The action plan may contain as few as two to three action steps or upward of six. It really just depends on the complexity of the skills that the student needs to improve. In the example provided, the deficit skill area is very specific and concrete—letter-naming fluency—so in this case, only two action steps are necessary.

TIME

This is simply the time allotted for the intervention. The number of days per week and minutes per day that are needed and allotted for each of the action steps should be clarified in this section of the template.

MATERIALS AND RESOURCES

Each time the student receives the intervention, the teacher or other professional should have all necessary materials and resources ready to go. Intervention time is often short periods of time; therefore, it is important that time is used wisely. If a teacher is unprepared with the necessary materials during this time, unnecessary time will be wasted.

PERSON RESPONSIBLE

This section of the template is very simple to complete. This is the name of the teacher, paraprofessional, or other education professional who will be working with the student to complete each action step. It is important to try to maintain consistency in this area each time the student meets for the defined intervention. The student will become comfortable working in a one-on-one or small group setting with that one teacher or professional and the way they approach instruction during this time period. It is helpful if that person is always the same.

Example:

Action Step	Time	Materials/ Resources	Person Responsible
Mark will receive ten minutes of small group intervention time to work on letter sound recognition each day.	10:10–10:20 Monday–Friday	• Letter cards • DIBELS letter sound fluency curriculum	Mrs. McKee, the general education kindergarten teacher
Mark will be assessed at the end of each week to monitor his progress toward his intervention objective.	10:15–10:20 Every Friday	• Letter cards • Letter sound fluency checklist	Ms. Dupont, the classroom aide

Interventions in the Content Areas

It is critical that once teachers identify the deficit skill area(s) of a student and determine the objective that needs to be met in order for the student to make progress toward grade-level mastery, appropriate research-based interventions are identified. The teacher or other professional must match the objective with an appropriate intervention. Utilizing reputable sources when looking for effective teaching methods, strategies, and programs is important. Below, you will find a chart for identifying helpful sources for making these matches. There are sources below that will be helpful when looking for intervention ideas in various content areas.

Content Area	Source	Where to Access This Information
Reading	1. The RTI Network	1. http://www.rtinetwork.org/essential/ tieredinstruction/tier1/effectiveteaching
	2. Reading Rockets	2. http://www.readingrockets.org/article/ best-practices-planning-interventions-students-reading-problems
	3. What Works Clearinghouse	3. https://ies.ed.gov/ncee/wwc/pdf/ practice_guides/rti_reading_pg_021809.pdf
	4. Best Evidence Encyclopedia	4. http://www.bestevidence.org/reading/ strug/top.htm
Writing	1. A Classroom Teacher's Guide to Struggling Writers	1. https://www.heinemann.com/ shared/onlineresources/E00765/ Dudley00765Sample.pdf
	2. Reading Rockets	2. http://www.readingrockets.org/article/ prevention-and-intervention-writing-difficulties-students-learning-disabilities
	3. Intervention Central	3. http://www.interventioncentral.org/ academic-interventions/writing/school-wide-strategies-managing-writing
Mathematics	1. Hanover Research Summary on Mathematics Interventions	1. https://www.mbaea.org/documents/ filelibrary/numeracy/Best_Practices_in_Math_Intervention_53D80FEED7650.pdf
	2. What Works Clearinghouse	2. http://ies.ed.gov/ncee/wwc/pdf/practice_guides/rti_math_pg_042109.pdf
	3. Intervention Central	3. http://www.interventioncentral.org/ academic-interventions/math/school-wide-strategies-managing-mathematics
Science	1. Reading Rockets	1. http://www.readingrockets.org/article/ using-technology-support-struggling-students-science-literacy-vocabulary-and-discourse
	2. Article by Sarah Carter	2. http://www.learnnc.org/lp/pages/7079
Social Studies	1. Reading Rockets	1. http://www.readingrockets.org/article/ supporting-reading-social-studies
	2. Social Studies Research and Practice	2. http://www.socstrpr.org/wp-content/ uploads/2013/01/06449_no8.pdf

Study Skills and Test-Taking Strategies	1. The Thoughtful Classroom	1. http://www.thoughtfulclassroom.com/PDFs/Isis-help-for-struggling-students.pdf
	2. Great Schools Website	2. http://www.greatschools.org/gk/articles/study-and-test-taking-strategies-for-kids-with-learning-difficulties/
	3. Songs that Teach Study Skills	3. http://www.songsforteaching.com/studytesttakingskills/
	4. LD Online	4. http://www.ldonline.org/indepth/study

Figure 4–1. Resource Chart for Interventions in the Content Areas

Conclusion

Overall, this chapter was designed to provide teachers with a plan of action for taking the information obtained about a student's deficit area(s) and developing it into a path to lead the student toward success through a specific intervention plan. The chapter reviewed the importance of the information included in each portion of the action plan template. Additionally, an example for how to complete each section of the action plan for your own student was included. At the conclusion of this chapter, the reader should be able to take this information and develop their own plan of action for a struggling learner they work with right now. The chapter wrapped up with a variety of sources to utilize to identify research-based interventions in various content areas. The following discussion questions and chapter activities can be used to further the progress made in working toward meeting the needs of all learners in today's classrooms.

Discussion Questions

These questions can be used as a basis for online discussion forums or as a starting point for discussion in the college classroom.

1. After reviewing the Intervention Action Plan template, respond to these questions: Have you used a process like this previously to be sure the students in your classroom that struggle have a clear path toward success? In the past, how did you determine what

intervention was appropriate for a student in need? Do you feel this template would be helpful in the process of providing interventions for your students?

2. Identify one of the recommended sources for assistance in identifying helpful interventions and teaching strategies for students struggling in the area of reading or writing. What information did this source provide? Summarize one type of intervention you learned about and post it to this week's discussion forum.

3. Identify one of the recommended sources for assistance in identifying helpful interventions and teaching strategies for students struggling in the area of mathematics. What information did this source provide? Summarize one type of intervention you learned about and post it to this week's discussion forum.

4. Identify one of the recommended sources for assistance in identifying helpful interventions and teaching strategies for students struggling in the area of science or social studies. What information did this source provide? Summarize one type of intervention you learned about and post it to this week's discussion forum.

5. Identify one of the recommended sources for assistance in identifying helpful interventions and teaching strategies for students struggling in the area of study skills or test taking. What information did this source provide? Summarize one type of intervention you learned about and post it to this week's discussion forum.

Chapter Activity

1. Choose a student from your own classroom that is in need of an intervention to address deficit skill area(s). Utilize the Intervention Action Plan template to develop a plan of action to support this student.

CHAPTER 5

A Multi-Tiered System of Support (MTSS) and the Response to Intervention (RTI) Model

Chapter Objectives

At the conclusion of the chapter, the reader will be able to:
- Define a multi-tiered system of support
- Identify the three key components of a multi-tiered system of support
- Define the Response to Intervention model
- Identify the core characteristics of the RTI model
- Describe the elements of Tiers 1, 2, and 3 on the RTI triangle

New Terminology

- MTSS
- RTI
- Standards-Aligned
- Standard Protocol Interventions

Introduction

This chapter was developed to provide an understanding of a multi-tiered system of support (MTSS) in a classroom, entire grade level, or school building. The qualities of an effective MTSS are discussed in this chapter. Additionally, the chapter will review in detail one research-based MTSS called Response to Intervention (RTI). The qualities and characteristics that make up the RTI framework will be reviewed in detail. Each of the tiers of support in the RTI system will be defined, and the implementation of each tier in a classroom or grade level is also presented.

Multi-Tiered System of Support

A multi-tiered system of support (MTSS) is defined as an integrated and comprehensive framework that focuses on core instruction, differentiated learning, meeting individual student needs, and standards-aligned curriculum that is necessary for all students' academic, behavioral, and social success (California Department of Education, 2015). This framework aligns an entire school building's set of initiatives, supports, and resources. The goal is to have a formalized system in place to access and utilize all the services available in a school building or district for any student that may be in need.

Additionally, MTSS focuses on continual improvement. As the needs of students change or increase, the MTSS model must expand to meet the needs of all learners in the classroom.

> *For example, if a group of migrant students that are English Language Learners move into the school district, the MTSS model will need to develop a support system to provide English as a Second Language instruction for the students and begin to plan for an initiative to help support the families of these new students as well.*

The Three Key Components of a Multi-Tiered System of Support

1. Address the needs of ALL learners.
2. Provide a framework that aligns all school initiatives, supports, and resources.
3. Implement continuous improvement at all levels of the system.

(California Department of Education, 2015, http://www.cde.ca.gov/ci/cr/ri/mtsscomprti2.asp)

The next section of this chapter provides an overview of the Response to Intervention (RTI) framework. RTI is an example of a tiered system of providing interventions. Consider MTSS a broader approach to meeting students' needs, characterized by those three main components: addressing the needs of all students by aligning the entire system of initiatives, supports, and resources, and by implementing continuous improvement processes at all levels of the system. However, the RTI model is a more specific model that focuses on meeting the academic needs of struggling learners through three tiers of instruction and intervention.

An Overview of Response to Intervention

Response to Intervention (RTI) is a comprehensive, standards-aligned school reform strategy that enables early identification and intervention for students needing additional opportunities to learn high-level content while providing on-level students the opportunity to make appropriate progress in the grade-level curriculum. RTI is used as a framework to provide quality, standards-aligned instruction to all students while also providing additional interventions through a three-tiered system that addresses the needs of all learners and makes sure no student falls through the cracks.

Additionally, RTI provides an alternate way to identify students with learning disabilities. By giving schools a clear structure of regular evaluation of student progress, the RTI model allows a student's progress to be clearly observed to determine if a student is consistently struggling and showing signs of a specific learning disability. Through the three-tiered model of RTI, struggling students are monitored closely as they receive research-based interventions. Data is tracked and decisions are made when interventions are not successful. If the student is still not making expected academic gains, all of this data can then be used to determine if they may qualify for special education services under the category of a specific learning disability. This process is used in place of the traditional special education evaluation process.

Do you feel using RTI to identify students with learning disabilities is more or less effective than the traditional special education evaluation process? Why?

_____

_____

It is important to remember that RTI not only provides interventions, but also provides the foundation of effective and necessary instruction for ALL students.

RTI is most effective when implemented school-wide or grade-wide, but it can also be effective when an individual teacher wants to utilize the framework in their own classroom. The recommendation is that RTI be used grade-wide or school-wide in order to have the greatest impact, so this chapter will outline how to implement this framework in the recommended context.

In your own words, define RTI:

_____

_____

TIER 1: THE FOUNDATION—STANDARDS-ALIGNED INSTRUCTION FOR ALL STUDENTS

RTI promotes the importance of effective instruction in building a strong core in that bottom tier of the triangle (see Figure 5.1). This is the most important tier of the RTI model. Consider Tier 1 the foundation of RTI. Within Tier 1, instruction must be standards-aligned to meet the requirements of federal and state standards and provide all students with access to instruction

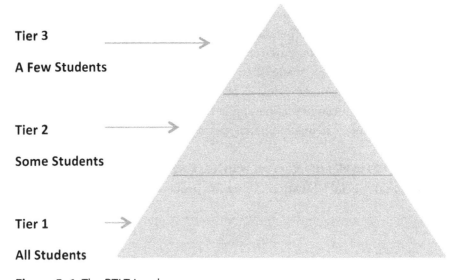

Tier 3

A Few Students

Tier 2

Some Students

Tier 1

All Students

Figure 5–1. The RTI Triangle

to meet those grade-level standards no matter what needs they may have. Some other characteristics of Tier 1 instruction are that the curriculum that is implemented is research-based, and lesson plans are made up of differentiated instruction activities and give students the opportunity to learn through multiple modalities.

During Tier 1 Instruction through RTI, assessment is critical. At the beginning of each school year, a universal screening tool is used to determine where all students are starting the year out in math and English language arts (reading and writing skills). This allows teachers to have a grade-level baseline for grade-wide goal setting. For example, by the second benchmark, 75% of second-graders will be at the benchmark in oral reading fluency. A teacher can then monitor class-wide progress, and this data can also be used to evaluate how effective the teacher's instruction or the curriculum may or may not be with this group of students. After analysis, the teacher may make changes to daily instruction, lesson planning, or curriculum.

This data can then be used to determine whether students are at risk for academic difficulties and in need of additional intervention time in Tier 2 or Tier 3. Within Tier 1, all students are also evaluated using a benchmark assessment three to five times throughout the school year. Again, this allows teachers the ability to see the impact of their instruction on the class as a whole group.

Within schools implementing RTI, it is recommended that grade-level teams are developed. For example, all five of the third-grade teachers in Strasburg Elementary School meet regularly to review benchmark data for their classes. The National Center for Learning Disabilities and the RTI Network recommend that grade-level teams meet within one week of the administration of the baseline assessment and future benchmark assessments given periodically throughout the school year. This allows teachers to analyze trends in the grade-level data in their schools as well as set grade-wide goals. They can also utilize the teaming approach to select appropriate research-based, grade-wide strategies to help reach identified grade-wide goals as well as brainstorm ideas for lesson planning, activities, and adjustment of the selected strategies.

What do you feel is the most important component of Tier 1 instruction?

TIER 2: INTERVENTIONS FOR SOME STUDENTS

Tier 2 intervention is provided in addition to the Tier 1 core program. Within the Tier 2 level of RTI, academic instruction, strategies, methodologies, and practices are implemented for some students in a classroom who are not making the progress expected within the Tier 1 core instruction and are considered at risk for academic failure. In Tier 2, students are grouped based on area of need and receive supplemental instructional time throughout each week to help get them back on track. The intervention time is provided on a consistent basis each week. The schedule of intervention time is provided daily, if possible, in addition to the time spent in the core instruction.

> *For example, if a fifth-grade classroom receives 90 minutes of English language arts instruction each day, the students in need of Tier 2 intervention time may receive an additional 15 minutes of small group instruction based on the skill area of need. In total each day, they would receive 105 minutes of instructional time in English language arts.*

The instruction in Tier 2 may be conducted by the general education teacher, but it is often done by a specialist—for example, a speech and language pathologist or a reading specialist. Additionally, students needing Tier 2 intervention may receive their small group instruction with students from other classes in the same grade level.

> *For example, in the third grade at Willow Street Elementary School, Mrs. Keesee may have four students needing Tier 2 intervention time to improve their reading fluency. Additionally, Mr. Decker may have two students in need of the same intervention. So the reading specialist, Ms. Harsh, may take these six students to her classroom each day for a fifteen-minute reading fluency lesson.*

Additionally, the instruction provided within Tier 2 is from research-based programs or strategies that have been proven effective with learners struggling in a specific skill area. If the program required a standard protocol or a standard set of requirements to implement the program effectively to receive the desired results, then the teacher or specialist working with this program must follow the protocol clearly and consistently. If the protocol requires that the student receive this type of instruction on a daily basis, then the teacher or specialist must make sure the student has a set time in their daily schedule to receive the intervention time.

> *For example, if the reading specialist, Ms. Harsh, wants to utilize the Read Naturally program with her six Tier 2 students from the third grade, then she must*

be willing to follow the Read Naturally protocol. This protocol requires the students have at least twenty to thirty minutes each day to be instructed using this program in order to receive the desired results that the program claims. (Read Naturally Protocol Manual, 2016)

Lastly, one of the key characteristics of Tier 2 intervention in the RTI model is that the students in this level of need are monitored on a regular basis for changes in their deficit skill area(s). The recommendation is that students are monitored every other week to determine if the intervention is working. It is also critical that we give the students time for the program to impact them. The RTI model recommends that no less than four data points are needed before determining if the student is making the necessary improvement to continue to implement that particular intervention with them. If four data points are necessary and the student is being assessed every two weeks, eight weeks of intervention time is necessary before determining whether the intervention is effective.

For example, Ms. Harsh begins using the Read Naturally program with her group of Tier 2 students in Week 1. She will monitor their progress through the program progress-monitoring tool every two weeks. At the end of Week 8, she can take a look at the data about each student to determine if this particular intervention program has been successful in helping each student make gains in their reading fluency.

If the data shows that after eight weeks of Tier 2 intervention time, the students are not making the gains necessary to get them back on track with their grade-level peers, then the grade-level teams (the teachers and specialists on the team who review RTI data from a specific grade level) will review the data and discuss each student individually. They will then decide if the student has made enough progress to go back to receiving only Tier 1 instruction, whether the student needs to continue with Tier 2 intervention time for a few more weeks, or whether the student is falling further behind and is in need of Tier 3 intervention time, which will be discussed in the next section of Chapter 4.

What do you feel is the most important component of Tier 2 instruction?

_____

_____

	Tier 1	Tier 2	Tier 3
Number of Students	Core instruction provided for ALL students	In addition to the Tier 1 core instruction for SOME students	In addition to the Tier 1 core instruction for a FEW students
Curriculum	Standards-aligned	Supplemental small group instruction	Small, intensive, flexible groups
Instruction	Research-based core program	Use of standard protocol interventions	Use of standard protocol interventions
Assessment	Benchmark assessment tool for all students three to five times per year	More frequent progress monitoring (every other week)	More frequent progress monitoring (every week)
Who	General education teachers	Specialists may assist with strategic instruction in general education classroom or in homogeneous skill group	

Figure 5–2. Characteristics of Instruction in Each Tier of RTI

TIER 3: INTERVENTIONS FOR A FEW STUDENTS

Tier 3 intervention is provided in addition to the Tier 1 core program. Within the Tier 3 level of RTI, academic instruction, strategies, methodologies, and practices are implemented for a few students in a classroom who are not making the progress expected within the Tier 1 core instruction and are also not making the expected gains in the Tier 2 level of intervention. These students are experiencing significant difficulties, are scoring significantly below grade-level benchmarks, and have not responded well to previously implemented interventions.

In Tier 3, students are grouped based on area of need and receive supplemental instructional time throughout each week to help get them back on track. The intervention time is provided on a consistent basis each week, and it typically increases from the amount of time spent in Tier 2 intervention. The schedule of intervention time is provided daily.

For example, if a second-grade classroom receives sixty minutes of mathematics instruction each day, the students in need of Tier 3 intervention time may receive an additional twenty minutes of small group instruction based on the skill area of need. In total each day, they would receive eighty minutes of instructional time in mathematics.

The instruction in Tier 3 is conducted by a specialist—for example, a speech and language pathologist, math coach, or a reading specialist. Additionally, students needing Tier 3 intervention may receive their small group instruction with students from other classes in the same grade level.

> *For example, in the second grade at George Washington Elementary School, Mrs. McIntosh may have one student needing Tier 3 intervention time to improve their knowledge of basic multiplication and division math facts. Additionally, Mr. Erickson may have two students in need of the same intervention. So the school's math coach, Ms. Anderson, may take these three students to her classroom each day for a twenty-minute math intervention lesson focused on math facts fluency.*

Additionally, the instruction provided within Tier 3 is from research-based programs or strategies that have been proven effective with learners struggling significantly in a specific skill area. If the program required a standard protocol or a standard set of requirements to implement the program effectively to receive the desired results, then the teacher or specialist working with this program must follow the protocol clearly and consistently. If the protocol requires that the student receive this type of instruction on a daily basis, then the teacher or specialist must make sure the student has a set time in their daily schedule to receive the intervention time.

> *For example, if the math coach, Ms. Anderson, wants to utilize the Pirate Math program with her three Tier 3 students from the second grade, then she must be willing to follow the Pirate Math protocol. This protocol requires the students have at least thirty minutes three days per week to be instructed using this program in order to receive the desired results that the program claims. (Fuchs, Powell, Seethaler, Cirino, Fletcher, et al., 2009)*

Lastly, one of the key characteristics of Tier 3 intervention in the RTI model is that the students in this level of need are monitored on a frequent and consistent basis for changes in their deficit skill area(s). The recommendation is that students are monitored every week to determine if the intervention is working. It is also critical that we give the students time for the program to impact them. The RTI model recommends that no less than four data points are needed before determining if the student is making the necessary improvement to continue to implement that particular intervention with them. If four data points are necessary and the student is being assessed every week, four weeks of intervention time is necessary before determining whether the intervention is effective.

> For example, Ms. Anderson begins using the Pirate Math program with her group of Tier 3 students in Week 1. She will monitor their progress through the program progress-monitoring tool each week. At the end of Week 4, she can take a look at the data about each student to determine if this particular intervention program has been successful in helping each student make gains in their math facts fluency.

If the data shows that after four weeks of Tier 3 intervention time, the students are not making the gains necessary to get them back on track with their grade-level peers, then the RTI grade-level teams (the teachers and specialists on the team who review RTI data from a specific grade level) will review the data and discuss each student individually. They will then decide if the student has made enough progress to go back to receiving only Tier 1 instruction, whether the student needs to continue with Tier 3 intervention time for a few more weeks, or whether the student is falling further behind and in need of evaluation to determine if the student qualifies for special education services through an Individualized Education Program (IEP).

What do you feel is the most important component of Tier 3 instruction?

_____

_____

IF STUDENTS DON'T DO WELL AT TIER 3 ...

If Tier 3 intervention time is not successful with a student, the student will then be considered for evaluation to determine if the student qualifies for special education services. At this time, the RTI grade-level team will request that this student be evaluated for special education services. The student's parents will then be contacted to seek permission to evaluate. Once this permission is received, the school psychologist will begin to collect information from the child's parents and teachers and assess the student to determine if they qualify for special education services.

If the child does qualify for special education at the conclusion of the evaluation process, the student will be assigned to a special education case manager, and an IEP will be developed based on that student's needs.

If the student does not qualify for special education services, then the RTI grade-level team will reconvene to discuss this particular student. They will develop a plan of action on how to make every effort to help this student make the necessary academic gains. The student will continue to participate in Tier 1 core instruction and receive additional support through the intervention tiers.

Conclusion

Throughout the RTI process, academic progress for each student remains the focus. Tier 1 provides a foundation for all students to receive core instruction that is aligned to the standards. Students are instructed using research-based strategies and curriculum that has been proven to be effective. Students are evaluated through a benchmark assessment three to five times per year to monitor students' growth. Grade-level teams are assigned to evaluate this data and look at trends within each grade level, classroom, and with each individual student.

Within Tiers 2 and 3, students are monitored even more closely through frequent assessment and have the opportunity to spend increased time with teachers or specialists in areas where they are struggling. This intervention time is provided in addition to the core instruction in Tier 1. The instruction provided within these tiers is also research-based and aligned specifically to the students' deficit skill areas.

Overall, the RTI process allows students the greatest chance for success. It provides a framework to meet the needs of all learners in the classroom. It provides teachers with a guide to the planning, instruction, and assessment to help each student in the classroom reach grade-level proficiency.

Discussion Questions

These questions can be used as a basis for online discussion forums or as a starting point for discussion in the college classroom.

1. Is an MTSS used in your school? If so, how are you involved in each tier of the RTI model? If you are not currently working in a school, have you seen RTI used during any of your field experiences?

2. Why do you feel it is important for grade-level teams to meet regularly to discuss students' progress at each level of the three tiers of RTI?

3. What programs does your school utilize for students in Tier 2 and Tier 3 who are struggling in the areas of mathematics and English language arts? Do you feel those programs are effective in meeting the needs of your students? If you are not currently working in a school, reflect on your field experiences; what programs have you seen used in Tier 2 and Tier 3 instruction? Do you feel they were effective?

4. Review the following websites and come up with a description of each and the helpful information provided on RTI. Post that to an online classroom discussion forum.

Chapter Activities

1. To test your understanding of the RTI model and its implementation, complete the RTI Case Study Activity at the end of this chapter.

Helpful Websites

- Center on Instruction: www.centeroninstruction.org/index
- What Works Clearinghouse: http://www.whatworks.ed.gov/
- Best Evidence Encyclopedia: www.bestevidence.org
- National Center on Response to Intervention: www.rti4success.org
- The RTI Action Network: http://www.rtinetwork.org/
- The IRIS Peabody Center: http://iris.peabody.vanderbilt.edu/iris-resource-locator/

RTI Case Study Activity

Scenario:

Tiffany is a third-grade student at Slippery Rock Elementary School. When Tiffany's teacher, Ms. McKee, administered the universal screening assessment in the area of reading during the fourth week of school, her score did not meet the benchmark in reading fluency. Because of this, Ms. McKee monitored Tiffany more closely by collecting data using the DIBELS reading fluency probes each week for six weeks. At the end of that time, Ms. McKee meets with her grade-level data analysis team to discuss Tiffany's progress.

Use the graph paper to:

1. Plot Tiffany's performance
2. Create a goal line based on the benchmark (in the fall of third grade, a student should score at 112 WCPM)
3. Calculate the slope of Tiffany's scores; the expected rate of growth should be at 1.4

Tiffany's Progress Monitoring Scores at Tier 1

Week 5	78
Week 6	79
Week 7	82
Week 8	81
Week 9	83
Week 10	84

What do you think the data analysis team decides about Tiffany's progress?

_____

_____

What conversation would you have with Tiffany's parents about her progress in your classroom? Please detail the dialogue you would have with them.

_____

_____

Based on the grade-level team meeting and the parent meeting, the decision is made to move Tiffany into a Tier 2 intervention group.

How many weeks will you administer a Tier 2 intervention before consulting with your grade-level data team to decide if Tier 2 is effective? _____

Why will you wait this amount of time?

_____

_____

CHAPTER 6

Meeting the Needs of All Learners through Differentiated Instruction

Chapter Objectives

At the conclusion of the chapter, the reader will be able to:
- Define the term differentiated instruction
- Identify four ways differentiated instruction can be applied to any classroom
- Recognize three principles that characterize a differentiated classroom
- Apply the framework of differentiated instruction to your own current or future classroom through application activities

New Terminology

- Differentiated Instruction
- Differentiation
- Learning Styles Inventory
- Kinesthetic

Overview of Differentiated Instruction

As classroom dynamics continue to become more diverse, it is important for educators to embrace a mission within their classrooms to meet the needs of a variety of learners in one classroom. To do this effectively, a teacher must be responsive to each learner's interest, style of learner, strengths, and weaknesses. Planning lessons that are interactive and address the various learning modalities is necessary. The technique that encourages teachers to plan, teach, and assess in this manner is called "differentiated instruction" or "differentiation."

Differentiated instruction is a framework to increase teacher effectiveness and student success by providing different students with different ways to learn in one classroom. It is very different than the one-size-fits-all approach to teaching that was historically implemented in many classrooms. Differentiation comes from the belief that each student is different in how they learn, their learning preferences, and individual interests, as well as their academic and behavioral strengths and weaknesses (Anderson, 2007).

Create your own definition of differentiated instruction here:

_____

_____

Differentiation is a proactive approach to teaching that encourages teachers to adjust teaching and learning methods to accommodate each child's needs and interests to increase their learning (Ellis, Gable, Greg, & Rock, 2008). There are four main ways that teachers can create this classroom environment.

Four Ways to Differentiate Your Classroom

- Content
- Process
- Product
- Environment

(Tomlinson, C., 1999)

CONTENT

The "What" that your students need to learn; the standards; the curriculum framework.

For example,

Ms. Houston is a first-grade teacher. Within her classroom this year, she has twenty-four students. Four of the students have learning disabilities and two students have intellectual disabilities. Ms. Houston utilizes differentiated instruction within her daily instruction to adjust the content of her lessons. She uses a parallel reading curriculum for her students with intellectual and learning disabilities. These students read about a similar topic as their peers (the students are all reading stories about a puppy), but their reading material is on a kindergarten level. During this week, these students are focusing on learning three new sight words that the rest of the class mastered in kindergarten.

In this example, Ms. Houston is differentiating the Content of her lesson to make sure that it is appropriate for all the learners in her classroom. Although these students are working on reading material at a different grade level, she is able to engage the entire class on discussion about the topic of the reading material.

What are some ways you can differentiate the content in your classroom?

_____

_____

PROCESS

The "How" of your instruction; what you will do as a teacher to engage the students in the lesson; the lesson plan activities.

For example,

Mr. Erickson is a sixth-grade teacher. In his classroom, he has twenty-six students. At the beginning of this school year, Mr. Erickson administers a learning styles inventory to all of his students. The inventory gives him information about the way that each of his students learn best. Based on this information, Mr. Erickson can now plan his lessons to include activities that address the different learning styles of his students. He has nine students in the classroom that learn best through kinesthetic (hands-on) activities based on the results from the learning style inventory. As a result, Mr. Erickson does his best to include hands-on activities in his mathematics lessons every day.

In this example, Mr. Erickson uses a learning styles inventory to gain more information about his students' learning strengths and preferences. He then takes that valuable information about his students and applies it to his classroom instruction. He is sure to address his students' various learning styles during his lessons to keep them engaged and help them to learn more effectively. Mr. Erickson is differentiating the Process of his classroom instruction.

What are some ways you can differentiate the process in your classroom?

_____

_____

Under the Chapter Activities section of this chapter, you will find links to three different learning styles inventories. Choose one and take it. What are the results? How would you use this information regarding your own students in the classroom?

_____

_____

PRODUCT

The "End Result" of your instruction; the final project; assessment that shows what a student has learned or mastered from the instruction.

For example,

Mr. Merhaut is a middle-school social studies teacher. In his current unit of instruction, he has been working with the students on their understanding of the Civil War. At the end of the unit, Mr. Merhaut gives each student a Think-Tac-Toe Board (see example in the Teacher Resources at the end of this chapter). Using the Think-Tac-Toe Board, the students are able to choose three activities to complete and submit for their end-of-unit grade. Each activity is different and allows the students to show mastery of the content in a different way.

In this example, Mr. Merhaut uses the Think-Tac-Toe board as the final project for the students to demonstrate mastery of the unit on the Civil War. The Think-Tac-Toe board allows students to choose three assessments to show their mastery. The activities are all different and allow the students to make choices based on their interests and strengths. Mr. Merhaut is differentiating the Product of his instruction through utilizing this assessment tool.

What are some other ways you can differentiate the product in your classroom?

_____

_____

ENVIRONMENT

The classroom "Setup"; the layout of the classroom; how the classroom feels.

For example,

Mrs. Risk is a kindergarten teacher. She embraces the framework of differentiation in her classroom and enjoys allowing her students to engage in activities that address their learning styles. As a result, her classroom environment is very collaborative. Students participate in a variety of small group, whole group, and individualized activities. In order to be conducive to these activities, Mrs. Risk has learning centers set up around her classroom to allow for small group, hands-on activities. Additionally, she has a large rug in the front of the room for whole group instruction and a quiet space with carpet squares for students to engage in individual time to read or listen to stories on tape.

In this example, Mrs. Risk creates a classroom environment that embraces differentiation. She has her classroom arranged to specifically allow for a variety of instruction and activities to occur. As a result, Mrs. Risk's students are able to learn in a variety of different groupings and learning styles, which helps to increase student engagement and skill mastery.

What are some ways you can differentiate the environment in your classroom?

_____

_____

How do you currently have your classroom set up to encourage differentiation? How might you change the layout to allow students greater opportunity to engage in flexible grouping activities?

If you are not yet teaching in a classroom, what classroom layouts have you observed during your field placements? How might you change these layouts to encourage more differentiation?

_____

_____

THREE PRINCIPLES OF A DIFFERENTIATED CLASSROOM

Within any differentiated classroom, there are three common characteristics that can be easily observed. The first is creating a classroom atmosphere that is flexible. Secondly, utilizing ongoing assessments of students' needs, and lastly, creating various types of student groupings all help to create a differentiated classroom environment. Each of these principles allows a classroom to give every student the opportunity to grow and learn based on their own individual strengths, needs, and learning preferences.

1. **The atmosphere in a differentiated classroom is flexible.**

In a differentiated classroom, a teacher embraces a flexible classroom environment. Various activities, learning centers, student groupings, and assessment types occur each day. When a student walks into that classroom each day, they feel welcomed into a learning environment that is fun and exciting.

What characteristics make your classroom flexible?

_____

_____

2. **Consistent, valuable assessment of a student's learning occurs continuously in a differentiated classroom.**

In a differentiated classroom, students are assessed often to be sure they are making adequate progress and responding well to each learning opportunity. Additionally, students are assessed using different assessment tools. In addition to traditional paper-and-pencil assessments, students are regularly given the chance to be assessed through non-traditional assessments like portfolios, journals, presentations, and oral discussions. The Think-Tac-Toe assessment tool is an example of this (see the section on Differentiating the Product in your classroom presented earlier in this chapter for more information). In a differentiated classroom, formative assessments are also used greatly. Formative assessments are frequent, ongoing assessments that are used to evaluate whether a student is engaged, comprehending, and moving toward mastery during daily instruction. Assessment tools like a simple thumbs up-thumbs down sign from the student if they understand a skill being presented is considered a formative assessment. Also, a graphic organizer or Ticket Out the Door are other examples of formative assessments. To see examples of these, turn to the Chapter Discussion Questions and Activities at the conclusion of this chapter.

What types of non-traditional assessments do you use in your classroom?

_____

_____

3. **Flexible grouping is a main staple in a differentiated classroom.**

In a differentiated classroom, a teacher is often strategic and purposeful in the groupings of students for various activities. A teacher may choose to group students based on ability for some activities while other times having students work in mixed-ability groups. Other times, groupings of students may be chosen based on students' academic or behavioral needs or based on their learning styles or interests.

Mixed-Ability Groups: Students of various academic levels working in the same group.

Similar-Ability Groups: Students of similar ability levels working in the same group.

Random Groups: The teacher groups students at random. No method is used to determine which students work together.

Additionally, it is important that a teacher in a differentiated classroom continuously utilize different types of groupings throughout the school day. Sometimes students may be seated in individual seats for group instruction but then moved into strategically chosen pairs for a reading activity, and then all come together to be seated on the carpet for a large group activity. The key is that the room groupings are flexible and change often to the meet the various needs and interests of the students.

What types of student groupings do you use most frequently in your classroom and why?

_____

_____

(The three principles reviewed in this chapter have been adapted from the work of Carol Ann Tomlinson in various publications and textbooks.)

Conclusion

In conclusion, embracing the philosophy of differentiated instruction is critical for today's teachers. Teachers today must be willing and able to respond to the academic, social, and behavioral needs of each of their students. Applying the Four Ways to Differentiate (Content, Process, Product, and Environment) into daily instruction is a valuable way to create a differentiated classroom. Additionally, adopting the Three Principles of a Differentiated Classroom (a flexible atmosphere, consistent, valuable assessment, and the use of flexible groupings) are also critical in creating a classroom setting that embraces each student's individual differences and allows for students to individually meet their greatest potential. Overall, every general education classroom must embrace these components in order to give each student the opportunity for success. Just remember, as a teacher, your role is to create an environment that allows for maximum student growth and success.

Discussion Questions

1. Based on the content of Chapter 6, are there any other principles that you feel are important in a differentiated classroom?

2. What ways do you address the needs of your students in the classroom through the Content, Process, Product, and Environment in your lessons? Give an example of one in each area.

3. What is your favorite way to group your students in the classroom? What kind of activities do the students complete while in this grouping?

4. Do you agree that formative assessments are important in the classroom? Why or why not?

5. How might you use a non-traditional type of assessment, such as portfolios, in your classroom?

Chapter Activities

1. Use the links to various learning styles inventories to administer one inventory of your choice to your students. Analyze the results with your students to help them discover their own learning style and so you can tailor your instruction to meet their learning styles. If you are not currently teaching, take one of the learning style inventories yourself. What kind of learner are you? Consider how this may impact your past or present educational experiences.
   - **Kolb's Learning Style Inventory (LSI):** http://psychology.about.com/od/educationalpsychology/a/kolbs-learning-styles.htm

- **Fleming's VARK Learning Style Questionnaire:** http://psychology.about.com/od/educationalpsychology/a/vark-learning-styles.htm
- **Online Learning Style Quiz Based on the VARK Model:** http://homeworktips.about.com/library/quizzes/bl_lstylequiz1.htm

2. Using the blank Think-Tac-Toe form located at thte end of this chapter, come up with a Think-Tac-Assessment that you could use in your own classroom based on a unit of instruction from your curriculum. Check out the Dare to Differentiate website at https://daretodifferentiate.wikispaces.com/file/detail/Think%20Tac%20Toe.ppt to see how to create your own Think-Tac-Toe board. Use the blank template provided to create one to use in your classroom.

3. Classroom Layout Activity: Using the handout and rubric describing the Differentiated Classroom Layout Activity, design your classroom with desks, tables, centers, and materials organized in a way conducive to differentiated instruction.

4. Graphic Organizer Activity: Describe and develop a graphic organizer that you would use to assess your students' learning during a reading comprehension activity. See the example provided at the end of this chapter as well as many other templates to create your own at the Enchanted Learning website: http://www.enchantedlearning.com/graphicorganizers/.

5. Ticket Out the Door Activity: Develop a "Ticket Out the Door" that you could use to evaluate your students' learning at the end of a lesson you recently taught. Check out the example provided at the end of this chapter.

Blank: Think-Tac-Toe Board
Corresponds with Chapter Activity #2

Unit Title:		
Think-Tac-Toe Activity		

Differentiate Classroom Layout Activity
Corresponds with Chapter Activity #3

Designing Your Differentiated Classroom
Sample Assignment Description
Worth 20 points

1. Choose a partner
2. Gather the materials you will need
3. Review the rubric
4. Use the web to brainstorm the key elements of your differentiated classroom
5. Utilizing the poster paper provided, design your differentiated classroom setup
6. Address areas covered below as part of your classroom setup. You should also provide a label and short description of interventions occurring in a given area (you can expand these in the question on the final page of the assignment).

   Example: Computer desks: - supports visual and hands-on learning
7. Complete the questions on the last page of the assignment

———————————————

Important elements (covered in Chapter 6) to keep in mind when designing your classroom setup:

- Four key elements of differentiated instruction
  - 1. Content
  - 2. Process
  - 3. Product
  - 4. Environment
- Three principles of differentiation
  - 1. The atmosphere in a differentiated classroom is flexible.
  - 2. Consistent, valuable assessment is used to evaluate student learning.
  - 3. Flexible grouping is used frequently.

Names: _____

Classroom Layout Reflection Questions

1. How does your classroom allow for effective organization? List three ways you planned for this in your classroom setup.

   _____

   _____

   _____

2. How does your classroom allow for you to address the learning styles of various students in the classroom? List three ways you planned for this in your classroom setup.

   _____

   _____

   _____

3. How does your classroom allow for flexible grouping? List three ways you planned for this in your classroom setup.

   _____

   _____

   _____

Differentiated Classroom Layout Activity
Rubric

Teacher Name: _____

Student Name: _____

Category	4	3	2	1
Organization	The poster includes various methods of organization that are conducive to a differentiated classroom.	The poster includes at least two methods of organization that are conducive to a differentiated classroom.	The poster includes minimal methods of organization.	This element is missing from the classroom arrangement.
Flexible Grouping	The poster includes a setup that allows for a variety of student grouping options that are conducive to a differentiated classroom.	The poster includes a setup that allows for at least two student grouping options that are conducive to a differentiated classroom.	The poster includes a setup that allows for minimal student grouping options.	This element is missing from the classroom arrangement.
Learning Styles	The poster includes a setup that allows for a variety of student learning styles that are conducive to a differentiated classroom.	The poster includes a setup that allows for at least two student learning styles that are conducive to a differentiated classroom.	The poster includes a setup that allows for minimal student learning style needs.	This element is missing from the classroom arrangement.
Attractiveness	The classroom layout is very attractive in terms of design, layout, and neatness.	The classroom layout is attractive in terms of design, layout, and neatness.	The classroom layout is acceptably attractive, though it may be a bit messy.	The poster is distractingly messy or very poorly designed.
Grammar	There are no grammatical/spelling mistakes on the poster.	There is one grammatical/spelling mistake on the poster.	There are two grammatical/spelling mistakes on the poster.	There are more than two grammatical/spelling mistakes on the poster.

Total Points: _____ /20

Comments:

Sequence of Events Story Map

Title: _____

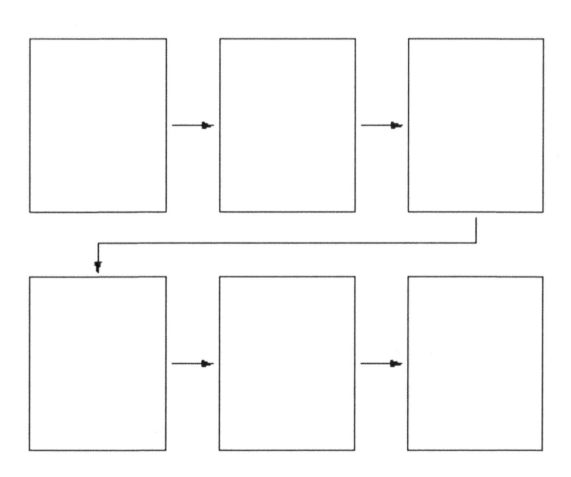

3-2-1 Ticket Out the Door

3 Things You Learned from Today's Lesson:
1.
2.
3.

2 Questions You Still Have:
1.
2.

1 Connection You Made from Today's Lesson to Something You've Learned Before:
1.

CHAPTER 7

Planning for Instruction

Chapter Objectives

At the conclusion of the chapter, the reader will be able to:
- Identify the eight key components of an Effective Core Instruction Lesson Plan
- Identify the four key components of an Intervention Lesson Plan
- Review a sample lesson plan template

New Terminology

- Anticipatory Set
- Direct Instruction
- Guided Practice
- Independent Practice

Introduction

As we reviewed the importance of quality core instruction in the general education for all learners in Chapter 3, it is imperative that the planning of lessons for the whole classroom incorporate a few key components. This chapter will review these components as well as look at a lesson plan template to be used with the general education classroom.

Additionally, in order to conduct effective instruction for students that require intervention time to support them as they reach mastery of skills, teachers must skillfully develop short, engaging lessons that hone in on the deficit skill area. The same lesson template will be reviewed, but with additional components important for teachers to incorporate in the lesson plans designed for small groups of students requiring interventions.

Components of an Effective Core Lesson Plan

1. Aligned to grade-level standards
2. An interesting anticipatory set
3. Direct instruction that includes differentiated instruction
4. Guided practice
5. Independent practice
6. Closure
7. Materials and resources
8. Assessment

ALIGNED TO GRADE-LEVEL STANDARDS

Lesson plans developed to meet the needs of diverse learners within the general education classroom must firstly be aligned to grade-level state standards. In the United States, these state standards must also align with the Common Core Standards that were adopted by individual states beginning in 2010. The foundation for a lesson plan is the standards that will be used to make sure the lesson content or curriculum align with the requirements for skill mastery in each grade level. Typically, lesson plans will require objectives that are created after reviewing the lesson standards and developing an objective that is measurable for each student at the lesson's conclusion. The remaining components of the lesson plan can only be developed after the standards of focus are identified and objectives are created.

ANTICIPATORY SET

Once the standards are determined, the planning of the lesson sequence begins. The start of the lesson sequence is the anticipatory set. The anticipatory set can be defined as a short portion of the lesson at the very beginning that is used to get the students' attention, activate their prior knowledge, and prepare them for the focus of today's lesson. Sometimes the anticipatory set is called the attention grabber or advance organizer for the lesson. It is important that the anticipatory set prepares the students' minds for the focus of the lesson but that it also gets them interested and excited about the lesson.

Give an example of an anticipatory set that you've used to get students excited about a lesson:

_____

_____

DIRECT INSTRUCTION

Direct instruction is the portion of the lesson that focuses on teacher instruction. At this point, the teacher will develop lesson steps that embrace the use of differentiated instruction to teach students a new skill. These steps are clearly written and follow a systematic way of introducing a new skill and leading students toward mastery of this new skill.

Direct instruction is also defined by the teacher or teachers (if working in a co-taught classroom) as being responsible for leading the instruction. It is often conducted in a full group setting, but sometimes cooperative groupings are used in different portions of the lesson sequence.

GUIDED PRACTICE

This portion of the lesson comes right after direct instruction on a specific skill area. At this point, the students have received instruction on a new skill. The next step in the lesson is to give the students the opportunity to practice the new learning under the direct supervision of their classroom teacher. The teacher leads the students through each step necessary to perform the new skill. This way, the teacher can catch the students making any errors immediately and guide the students in the correct direction so that they are able to demonstrate the new skill correctly.

INDEPENDENT PRACTICE

Following ample time with guided practice, the teacher will then move on to time for independent practice. This only occurs once the teacher is sure that the students understand the new material. At this time, the teacher releases the students to practice on their own based on the learning mastery that has occurred during the previous steps. Once students are successful at this point in the lesson, then it is time to move on to an assessment and then a new skill.

In your current classroom, do you typically utilize guided and independent practice activities? Why or why not?

_____

_____

CLOSURE

At the end of each lesson, the teacher reviews or wraps up the lesson. Sometimes the teacher will end the lesson by posing a question for the class: "Tell me what you have learned today." Closure is not necessarily an end point, but more of a final "check for understanding" used at the end of a class period. It is important to tie together your lesson before ending that instruction.

Sometimes teachers run short on time and the lesson ends during independent instruction time. This time is important to help students reflect on their own learning. Additionally, during the lesson closure, it is a good time for a teacher to reflect on the lesson objective and determine if sufficient information has been gathered about a student's progress on that particular objective. If it has not, the teacher can use the closure to ask specific questions to determine the student's skill mastery.

MATERIALS AND RESOURCES

Materials and resources are any items like books, handouts, graphic organizers, markers, crayons, etc. that a teacher will need to teach students the skills outlined in the lesson plan. It also includes the use of certain websites or technology tools like a SmartBoard, iPad, or particular iPad applications.

List some unique materials you've used in lesson plans that help students master new skills and allow them to have fun at the same time:

_____

_____

What kind of technology do you use in your lessons each day?

_____

_____

ASSESSMENT

Based on the objective(s) written from the identified standards for the lesson, students should each be evaluated to determine whether they met mastery of the lesson objective(s). This is when an assessment is necessary. The teacher may simply use observation to determine a student's mastery of an objective or a more traditional type of assessment may be used. For example, a quiz, handout, or graphic organizer may all be used to determine how well a student mastered the objective. Many types of assessments may be utilized, but it's important to make sure the lesson objectives and the assessments match up and that data is then used to develop the content for upcoming lessons.

Review the lesson plan template included at the end of this chapter. How does this template differ from ones you've seen or used previously? What is similar or different between the various lessons? What do you like about this template?

_____

_____

Components of an Effective Intervention Lesson Plan

1. Frequency
2. Focus of instruction
3. Format of lesson
4. Size of group

Although the lesson plan template introduced in this lesson can be used for both a full group general education lesson as well as a small group or individualized intervention lesson, there are some items that must be emphasized when focusing on a group of struggling learners during intervention time. Those four components will be explained further in this section of the chapter.

FREQUENCY

The frequency of an intervention lesson refers to how often the skills will be addressed each week. With interventions, students are often instructed in these deficit areas for smaller chunks of time on a consistent basis. Frequency of these types of lessons is critical. This must be determined prior to the intervention time beginning, and this must stay consistent throughout the week.

FOCUS

The second component of intervention lessons that needs to be carefully considered is the lesson focus. After determining that a student is in need of an intervention to improve a deficit skill area, a very clear focus for the intervention time can be determined. Within an intervention lesson, the lesson standards and objectives will be very specific and directly aligned to the skill area that was used to determine the student's need for an intervention. A student may actually be working on the same lesson objective every day for a week or more. This focus will remain consistent for each intervention lesson until the student can demonstrate mastery.

FORMAT

Within an intervention lesson, the format may be different. Although direct instruction, guided practice, and independent practice are important in these lessons, you may find that they are not appropriate for every lesson. A teacher may develop a twenty minute reading lesson focused on improving a student's oral reading fluency. Within that particular type of lesson, the teacher may only use a brief time of direct instruction and then spend the remaining time with guided practice. The format of intervention lessons relates directly to the deficit skill areas and the individual student needs.

GROUP SIZE

In an intervention lesson plan, the group size is significantly smaller. In a typical general education lesson, group sizes may range from fifteen to thirty students. However, in an intervention lesson, students are grouped by very specific needs. Typically, the groups of students that may have similar needs should remain small. Groups of not more than five to six students are often most appropriate for this type of lesson. There are times that an intervention lesson may be written specifically for just one student. Again, this all depends on the individual needs of the student. The ultimate goal is to help each student to reach mastery and do whatever it takes to get them to that point.

Conclusion

This chapter focused on the importance of developing lesson plans that are effective for a full classroom of students in the general education classroom as well as for a small number of students with specific needs in an intervention lesson. This chapter reviews in clear and concise terms the necessary components to both types of lesson plans. Additionally, the lesson plan template provided gives teachers a clear tool to utilize with their own students. You will also find in the chapter activities various scenarios that could be used as you practice writing lessons using this template. Choose one and give it a try.

Discussion Questions

These questions can be used as a basis for online discussion forums or as a starting point for discussion in the college classroom.

1. Given the lesson plan template at the end of this chapter, how might this template work well for general education teachers as well as for other professionals working with groups of struggling learners during intervention time?

2. Using the scenario listed below, get creative. Practice writing a lesson plan to address the specific needs of these students using the template provided.

Chapter Activity

1. Using the lesson plan template provided, develop a scenario based on the information provided below:

INTERVENTION LESSON PLAN SCENARIO

- You have given a benchmark assessment in mathematics to all of your first-grade students during the second week of school.
- You have found that a group of three to five students in your classroom have scored below the benchmark. One specific area of struggle is in understanding of place value from the standards under the area of Numbers and Operations.
- Develop a lesson utilizing the lesson plan format provided in this chapter. Focus your lesson plan on the understanding of place value. You have twenty minutes each day to provide intervention time for students struggling in mathematics, so plan your lesson for this block of time.

LESSON PLAN TEMPLATE

To be used with general education lessons and intervention lessons for small groups of struggling learners:

Teacher(s) Name:
Grade Level:
Content Area:
Lesson Topic:
Date and Time Allotted:
Audience (Identify if this is a general education lesson or small group lesson):

Objective #	State Standard	Condition	Behavior	Degree	Evaluation
	Include standard code and wording for the standard	Under which the behavior will be performed	Exhibited by students as a result of the lesson	Of accuracy needed for mastery	Of student performance. How will data be collected? Attach checklists, handouts, and/ or forms to lesson plan.
Example:	Third-Grade Pennsylvania State Math Standard: CC.2.2.3.A.3 Demonstrate multiplication and division fluency.	Given a two-digit multiplication quiz,	The student will respond accurately	To 80% or more of the questions	As determined through the multiplication quiz answer key graded by the classroom teacher.

Lesson Materials and Resources

Lesson Sequence:	Time Allotted for this step:	Teacher will:	Student(s) will:	Any accommodations or modifications needed for particular students:
Anticipatory Set				
Direction Instruction				

Guided Practice			
Independent Practice			
Closure/Lesson Wrap-Up			

Assessment (How will student be evaluated for mastery of the objectives listed above?):

**All materials needed in the lesson must be attached to the lesson, including handouts, graphic organizers, and assessment tools used to collect data.

CHAPTER 8

Co-Teaching and Its Models

Chapter Objectives

At the conclusion of the chapter, the reader will be able to:
- Define the term co-teaching
- Identify the five models of co-teaching presented in this chapter
- Determine common strengths and weaknesses when using each co-teaching model in the classroom

New Terminology

- Co-Teaching
- Team Teaching
- Parallel Teaching
- Stations Teaching
- One Teach, One Assist

Introduction

Co-teaching has been around for many years in classrooms across the country. It has been used to provide better supports for teachers and their students as teachers work hard to support the diverse needs of their class roster. This chapter looks at co-teaching as a teaching strategy effective in addressing the needs of students discussed in many of the chapters throughout the text. This chapter will review the various co-teaching models proven effective in the classroom as well as the strengths and weakness of each. Additionally, the chapter concludes with multiple discussion questions, which encourage the reader to consider their own classroom experiences and the use of co-teaching to increase student achievement within those experiences.

CO-TEACHING

Richael Barger-Anderson, Robert Isherwood, Joseph Merhaut

Credit: Richael Barger-Anderson, Robert Isherwood, and Joseph Merhaut, "Co-Teaching," *Strategic Co-Teaching in Your School Using the Co-Design Model*, pp. 111-122. Copyright © 2013 by Paul H. Brookes Publishing Co., Inc. Reprinted with permission.

Models of Co-Teaching

Several definitions for co-teaching exist. However, for implementation of the Co-Design Model, the authors have chosen the definition provided by Marilyn Friend (2007). Co-teaching is a way for two professionals to provide specially designed instruction to students with disabilities. It affords access to the general education curriculum in the LRE with appropriate supplemental aids and services. Both professionals share the physical space of the classroom, take ownership of sharing all students, and are respectful of each other's skill sets and training (Cook & Friend, 1996; Friend, 2011).

Professionals who may be assigned to co-teaching include general education teachers; special education teachers; special teachers such as librarians; physical education, computer, art, and music teachers; reading specialists; literacy and math coaches; and therapists (e.g., speech-language, physical, and occupational therapists). Note that paraprofessionals are not in this list. Although the role of the paraprofessional is quite important in today's classroom, the affiliation between the paraprofessional and the teacher is not one of co-teaching. The role of the paraeducator is addressed later in this chapter.

We define the practice of co-teaching as shared collaborative educational practices between two or more professionals (Barger-Anderson, Isherwood, & Merhaut, 2010). For this pathway to be used successfully, teachers and paraprofessionals must receive training about co-teaching models and about the district's expectations. It is also important for partners in the collaborative environment to realize that co-teaching will be supported through resources other than a "one-shot" training experience. [...]

Marilyn Friend recognizes six models in her research. In the Co-Design Model the authors advocate the use of five of these models (Friend, 2007):

1. One teach/one assist
2. Stations
3. Parallel
4. Alternative
5. Team

Table 8.1 is an overview and visual depiction of the live models of co-teaching promoted in the Co-Design Model. (Friend's sixth model is one teach/one observe.)

A Closer Look at the Five Models

The five models of co-teaching offered by Friend (2005, 2007) provide teachers with a systematic approach for implementing shared instructional practices. To assist with the implementation of successful co-teaching, Keystone Educational Consulting Group has created a Co-Teach Lesson Plan form. [...] This lesson plan form allows teachers to designate which model of co-teaching will be implemented and helps them assign roles to promote active participation of both teachers. The remainder of this section describes the five models and provides a sample lesson plan for each.

1. In the one teach/one assist model, one professional serves as the main facilitator or provider of knowledge; the other professional serves as the assistant (Figure 8.1). The assistant may help promote on-task behavior, answer individual questions posed by students, assist with housekeeping duties, implement behavior plans, and prompt and cue as necessary. There are a variety of ways to use the professional serving as the assistant in a meaningful manner. However, repeated use of this model of co-teaching rarely results in productive use of the other professional. Many times, over implementation of this model results directly in the deprofessionalization of the other teacher.

Table 8-1. Overview of co-teaching models

Model	Definition	Visual depiction
One teach/ one assist	One professional serves as the main facilitator/provider of knowledge, while the other professional serves as the assistant. The assistant may help promote on-task behavior, answer individual questions posed by students, assist with housekeeping duties, implement behavior plans, and so forth. There are a variety of ways to use the professional serving as the assistant in a meaningful manner.	X O O O O O O O O O O O O O O O O O O O O X
Stations	The classroom is divided Into student groups of three or more. Each professional is responsible for the learning that occurs at one of the stations, while one or more of the stations are devised to run independently of a teacher. A paraprofessional may assist with a station as long as no direct instruction is being provided. The students may rotate through the stations within the class period.	O O O X O O O O O O O O O O X O O
Parallel	The class is divided into two equal parts. Once the class has been divided, each professional is responsible for instruction for one group. Each teacher is providing the same content to each group of students. The benefit of this model is the decrease in student-teacher ratio.	X O O O O O O O O X
Alternative	Professionals are encouraged to "think outside the box" for this model. The alternative model promotes large-group instruction for the majority of the class, while a small group of students receives instruction in an alternative location (either within the classroom or outside the classroom). Teachers are encouraged to trade responsibility for teaching the large group and to keep the composition of the small group flexible.	X O O O O O O O O O O O O X O O O O
Team	In team teaching, both teachers share the stage. Team teaching is a collaborative effort between two professionals to provide or facilitate instruction to a whole group of students. Given time, this model may be very rewarding. Trust must be established between the two teachers before the team model yields the greatest benefits.	X X O O O O O O O O O O O O O O O O

Sources: Friend (2005, 2007).

Key: X, teacher; O, student.

CO-TEACH LESSON PLAN

Co-teachers: Ms. Lime and Ms. Barbosa	Date: Jan. 11	Room: 204	Day: Tuesday	Grade: 5	Time/period: 3rd period	Subject: Language Arts

Co-teaching model: X One teach/one assist   _ Parallel
     _ Stations   _ Team
     _ Alternative   _ Other
	Co-plan time:
	1/6 10:15–11:15 a.m.

State standard	Short-term objectives	Evaluation
1.2.5 D	**1.** Using a know-want-Learn (KWL) chart, the students will identify what they already know, what they want to know, and what they have learned about the Chinese zodiac during this lesson. Each column will have a minimum of three entries. **Modifications:**	Completed KWL chart
1.6.5 D	**2.** While being read a story aloud, students will participate in oral questioning while listening to the story. Each student must answer at least one time when called upon. **Modifications:** Students may ask a peer for assistance when answering the questions.	Observation and checklist
1.6.5 C	**3.** Using the packet of materials provided, the students will orally identify their zodiac sign and complete an animal outline with at least three accurate facts. **Modifications:**	Observation and completed animal outline
	4. Given time in class, students must orally present their animal to the class and share at least two reasons why or why not the animal is a good descriptor of them. **Modifications:** Students may practice what they are going to share with the class with a teacher before presenting to the class.	Observation and checklist
Materials: The Animals of the Chinese Zodiac, KWL chart, Chinese zodiac packets, markers, book, pencils		**Other:**
Introduction: *Teacher responsible:* Ms. Lime	Teacher will introduce a KWL chart. Together teacher and students will complete the K(know) section of the chart with prior knowledge about the Chinese zodiac and the W (what they want to learn) section of the chart with what they would like to know about the Chinese zodiac.	

(*Continued*)

Figure 8–1. Co-teaching example: one teach/one assist model. (Copyright © 2013 by Keystone Educational Consulting Group. Reprinted with permission.)

Lesson sequence: Teacher responsible: Ms. Barbosa	Read the book <u>The Animals of the Chinese Zodiac</u> by Susan Whitfield to the class. Teacher will provide packets to the students with information on the zodiac and explain how to identify the animal that matches their date and year of birth. Students will work in pairs to locate the animals that matches their birth date and year. They will be given an outline of their animal and write at least three descriptors of the animal inside the outline.
Closing: Teacher responsible: Ms. Lime	Students will each share their Chinese zodiac animal with the class. They will share whether they think the animal's description is a good description of themselves. The students must share why or why not. Students will complete the L (what they Learned) section of the KWL chart.
Homework: Teacher responsible to assign: Ms. Lime Teacher responsible to correct: Ms. Lime	The students will find the Chinese zodiac sign of at least three family members or friends.
Reflections:	

Figure 8–1. (*continued*)

2. In the stations model, the classroom is divided into groups of three or more students. Each professional is responsible for the planning, implementation, and assessment of learning that occurs at one of the stations, while one or more of the stations are devised by the co-teachers to run independently of a facilitator (Figure 8.2). A paraprofessional may assist with a station as long as no direct instruction of new content is being provided. (Again, the role of paraprofessionals in relation to co-teaching is addressed later in this chapter.) The students rotate from station to station throughout the class period. If behavior or concerns with student transitions from station to station cause trepidation, the teachers may move while the students remain in place. A benefit of this model is a lower student-teacher ratio. Also, different learning modalities may be addressed at each of the stations. Use of this model increases engagement time of students within each station.

3. In the parallel model, the class is divided into two equal parts. Once the class has been divided, each professional is responsible for instruction of one group (Figure 8.3). A para-professional may be responsible for a group if new content is not being presented and the teacher has made the decisions for the content of the lesson. Each teacher is providing the same or similar content to each group of students. As in the stations model, one of

CO-TEACH LESSON PLAN

Co-teachers: Ms. Sparrow Ms. Bea	Date: Feb. 5	Room: 13	Day: Tuesday	Grade: 5	Time/period: 2nd period	Subject: Social Studies & Reading

Co-teaching model: _ One teach/one assist ___ Parallel X Stations ___ Team _ Alternative ___ Other	Co-plan time: 1/29 1:45–2:45 p.m.

State standard	Short-term objectives	Evaluation
1.3.5. Standard A	**1.** Using the packet of materials provided, students will guess and identify their animal in the Chinese zodiac. **Modifications:** Read material to students. Display a few characteristics of each animal on a PowerPoint slide show, to limit the amount of material the student needs to read. Teacher assistance to answer accuracy.	Checklist
1.4.5. Standard D	**2.** Individually, the students will complete a graphic organizer that compares/contrasts at least two zodiac animals. **Modifications:** Students may complete the graphic organizer in pairs.	Completed graphic organizer
1.6.5. Standard D	**3.** While being read a story aloud, students will participate in oral questioning while listening to the story. Each student must answer at least one time when called upon. **Modifications:** Students may ask a peer for assistance.	Observation and checklist
	4. **Modifications:**	
Materials: The Animals of the Chinese Zodiac, Chinese zodiac packets, story, graphic organizers, PowerPoint slide show, timer, pencils		**Other:**
Introduction: *Teacher responsible:* Ms. Bea	The students are asked to think about what animals they like best. The Chinese zodiac will be introduced. The students will guess which animal they think they are. The students will be divided into three groups and given directions and transition information for the station activities. When they hear the timer ring, it is time to switch stations.	

(*Continued*)

Figure 8–2. Co-teaching example: stations model. (Copyright © 2013 by Keystone Educational Consulting Group. Reprinted with permission.)

Lesson sequence: Teacher responsible: Ms. Bea Mr. Sparrow will facilitate both stations 2 and 3.	Station 1: Read the book <u>The Animals of Chinese Zodiac</u> by Susan Whitfield and orally discuss the contents throughout the reading and at conclusion. Bea will either read the book aloud or select a student(s) to read aloud.
	Station 2: Students will be provided with Chinese zodiac animal descriptions and select the animal that fits them the most characteristically. Once students have selected the animal, they must check their birth year and date with the Chinese zodiac to see if their prediction aligned with the correct animal. The teacher will show a PowerPoint slide show to help present the information if needed.
	Station 3: Students will be given a graphic organizer to complete. The students must select at least two animals to compare/contrast using the graphic organizer. The students may work individually at the station or in pairs.
Closing: Teacher responsible: Ms. Sparrow	The students will come together as a whole class for the closing. The teacher will ask the entire class a few questions about the activities from the stations:
	Recall questions about the book in station 1. How did you react when you found the actual animal that matched your date and year of birth? Did you guess correctly? What are your thoughts about the Chinese zodiac?
Homework: Teacher responsible to assign: Ms. Bea Teacher responsible to correct: Ms. Sparrow	Students will find the Chinese zodiac sign of at least three family members or friends.
Reflections:	

Figure 8–2. (*continued*)

the benefits of this model is the decrease in student-teacher ratio. A common complaint about this model is the increase in noise from two teachers speaking at the same time in one classroom. It is common for co-teachers to *not* succeed during the first trial of parallel co-teaching. Barger-Anderson, Isherwood, and Merhaut (2010) recommend trying this model at least two times before abandoning it. Other benefits from the use of this model include increased engaged time of students, the option to address various learning styles, and flexibility in grouping students.

4. In the alternative model, professionals are encouraged to "think outside the box." The alternative model promotes large-group instruction for the majority of the class, while a small group of students receives instruction in an alternative location (either within or outside the classroom). Teachers are encouraged to switch roles, trading responsibility for teaching the

CO-TEACH LESSON PLAN

Co-teachers: Mrs. Fletchter and Mr. Perry	Date: Jan. 25	Room: 13	Day: Monday	Grade: 5	Time/period: 12:30–1:30 p.m.	Subject: Social Studies, Reading & Language Arts

Co-teaching model: _ One teach/one assist X Parallel	Co-plan time:
_ Stations _ Team	1/11 3:30–4:30 p.m.
_ Alternative _ Other	

State standard	Short-term objectives	Evaluation
World language and culture 2.1	**1.** While being read a story aloud, students will participate in oral questioning while listening to the story. Each student must answer at least one time when called upon. **Modifications:** Students may ask a peer for assistance if needed.	Observation and checklist
Reading, writing, listening, speaking 1.4 Types of writing	**2.** Given Chinese zodiac packets, students will orally identify their Chinese zodiac sign. **Modifications:** Teacher assistance if needed.	Observation
Reading, writing, listening, speaking 1.5 Quality of writing 1.6 Speaking and listening	**3.** Given the Chinese zodiac packets, students will write three complete sentences about their Chinese zodiac sign. **Modifications:** Students will work in groups and will be able to revise their sentences with assistance from the teacher.	Sentences
2.5.5 Standard C	**4.** Given a bar graph and pieces of paper with their name, students will place their name in the correct space on the zodiac bar graph. **Modifications:** Teacher or peer assistance if needed.	Bar graph
Materials: <u>Celebrating Chinese New Year</u> (2 copies), Chinese zodiac packets, papers with names for bar graph, bar graph, paper to write sentences, pencils		**Other:**

(*Continued*)

Figure 8–3. Co-teaching example: parallel model. (Copyright © 2013 by Keystone Educational Consulting Group. Reprinted with permission.)

Introduction: Teacher responsible: Both teachers	The teacher will divide students into two equal-sized groups based on their ability levels. Each teacher will follow the steps in the Introduction, Lesson Sequence, and Closing with his or her group of students.
	Teacher will introduce Chinese culture by reading the book <u>Celebrating Chinese New Year</u> by Diana Hoyt-Goldsmith. The teacher will ask questions throughout the story to check for reading comprehension. The teacher will explain to students that they are going to find and learn about their Chinese zodiac sign.
Lesson sequence: Teacher responsible: Both teachers	Each student will review the Chinese zodiac packet to find his or her zodiac sign. Once each child determines his or her sign, the child will write at least three sentences about the characteristics for his or her sign on notebook paper. Students will share their sentences with their peers in their group to make grammatical corrections.
Closing: Teacher responsible: Both teachers	The teacher will tell students that a zodiac sign bar graph for the class has been created in the classroom. Each student will be given a piece of paper with his or her name on it. On their way out of class, they are to place their name in the appropriate zodiac sign category. The class will start the next day by looking at the results of the bar graph.
Homework: Teacher responsible to assign: Teacher responsible to correct:	There will be no homework assigned for this lesson and activity.
Reflections:	

Figure 8–3. (*continued*)

large group (Figure 8.4). The composition of the small group should remain flexible. Some days the small group may comprise students needing enrichment and another day those needing remediation. It may even comprise the students who were absent the day before. It is important to keep an open mind for this model and be creative with the use of student groupings. This model does not promote pulling the same students or routinely moving the students with an IEP to the back or side of the room to work only with the special education teacher. As in all the models, purposeful and data-driven decisions should determine the composition of the groups and the teacher responsible for the instruction.

5. Team teaching is equal sharing of the stage. Team teaching is a collaborative effort between two or more professionals to provide or facilitate instruction to a whole group of students (Figure 8.5). Given time, this model may be very rewarding. Trust must be established between the two teachers before the model can yields the greatest benefits. At the start, it

CO-TEACH LESSON PLAN

Co-teachers: Mrs. Findley Mr. Brady	Date: Feb. 17	Room: 205	Day: Monday	Grade: 5	Time/period: 9–10 a.m.	Subject: Language Arts

Co-teaching model: _ One teach/one assist _ Stations X Alternative	_ Parallel _ Team _ Other	Co-plan time: 2/8 2:15–3:15 p.m.

State standard	Short-term objectives	Evaluation
1.2.5	**1.** While being read a story aloud, students will participate in oral questioning while listening to the story. Each student must answer at least one time when called upon. **Modifications:** Students may ask a peer for assistance if needed.	Observation and checklist
1.5.5	**2.** Using the packet of materials provided, students will guess and identify their animal in the Chinese zodiac. **Modifications:** Read material to students. Display a few characteristics of each animal on a PowerPoint slide show, to limit the amount of material the student needs to read. Teacher assistance if needed to ensure accuracy.	Checklist
	3. Individually, the students will complete a graphic organizer that compares/contrasts at least two zodiac animals. **Modifications:** Students may work in pairs.	Graphic Organizer
	4. **Modifications:**	

Materials: <u>The Animals of the Chinese Zodiac</u>, Chinese zodiac packets, book (2 copies), graphic organizers, PowerPoint slide show, pencils	Other:

Introduction: *Teacher responsible:* Ms. Brady	Read the book <u>The Animals of the Chinese Zodiac</u> by Susan Whitfield to the class. The students are asked to think about what animals they like best. The students will guess which animal they think they are.

(*Continued*)

Figure 8–4. Co-teaching example: alternative model. (Copyright © 2013 by Keystone Educational Consulting Group. Reprinted with permission.)

Lesson sequence: *Teacher responsible:* Both teachers	Teachers will divide the students into two groups, one small and one large based on results of previously collected data. Ms. Brady will keep the large group of students, while Mr. Findley takes the small group of students to a work area at the side of the room. Both teachers will follow the steps in the Introduction, Lesson Sequence, and Closing with their group of students. All students will be provided with Chinese zodiac animal descriptions and select the animal that fits them the most characteristically. The teacher will show a PowerPoint slide show to help present the information if needed.
	Once students have selected their animal, they must check their birth year and date with the Chinese zodiac to see if their prediction aligned with their correct animal. Students will be given a graphic organizer to complete. The students must select at least two animals to compare/contrast using the graphic organizer. The students may work individually or in pairs.
Closing: *Teacher responsible:* Both teachers	The teachers will orally present the class a few questions: Recall questions about the book. How did you react when you found the actual animal that matched your date and year of birth? Did you guess correctly? What are your thoughts about the Chinese zodiac?
Homework: *Teacher responsible to assign:* Both teachers *Teacher responsible to correct:* Both teachers	Students will find the Chinese zodiac signs of at least three family members or friends.
Reflections:	

Figure 8–4. (*continued*)

may even help for the co-teachers to script questions to ask each other in front of the class. The back-and-forth between teachers may be a bit "clunky" at first; taking turns may be almost as formal as passing a baton. Over time, however, the goal is to achieve a seamless transition from teacher to teacher.

Application to the Shared Classroom

When considering co-teaching models, the collaborative partners need to first select which model to implement for which lesson and then, when necessary, decide how to group the students.

It is important for pairs to avoid overuse of the one teach/one assist model. Too often, this model is viewed as the "default" model. True, it is easy to implement and requires little

CO-TEACH LESSON PLAN

Co-teachers: Mr. Titan Mr. Gibbs	Date: Feb. 13	Room: 107	Day: Friday	Grade: 5	Time/period: 40 minutes	Subject English & Social Studies

Co-teaching model: _ One teach/one assist _ Parallel _ Stations X Team _ Alternative _ Other	Co-plan time: 2/7 8:15–9:30 a.m.

State standard	Short-term objectives	Evaluation
	1. While being read a story aloud, students will participate in oral questioning while listening to the story. Each student must answer at least one time when called upon. **Modifications:** Students may ask a peer for assistance when answering the questions.	Observation and checklist
1.4.3	**2.** Given packets on the zodiac signs, students will orally identify their Chinese zodiac sign. **Modifications:** Teacher assistance if necessary to ensure accuracy.	Observation
1.5.3	**3.** After identification of their sign, students will write three complete sentences about their Chinese zodiac sign. **Modifications:** Students may work in groups and will be able to revise their sentences with assistance from the teacher.	Sentences
2.5.5 Standard C	**4.** Given a bar graph and pieces of paper with their name, students will place their name in the correct space on the zodiac bar graph. **Modifications:**	Bar graph

Materials: Book: Celebrating Chinese New Year, Chinese zodiac packets, papers with names for bar graph, bar graph, paper to write sentences, pencils	Other:

Introduction: *Teacher responsible:* Both teachers	Teacher will introduce Chinese culture by reading the children's book Celebrating Chinese New Year by Diana Hoyt-Goldsmith. The teacher will ask questions throughout the story to check for reading comprehension. The teachers will explain to students that they are going to find and learn about their Chinese zodiac sign.

(*Continued*)

Figure 8–5. Co-teaching example: team model. (Copyright © 2013 by Keystone Educational Consulting Group. Reprinted with permission.)

(Continued)

Lesson sequence: *Teacher responsible:* Both teachers	Teachers review the Chinese zodiac packet to find the student zodiac sign. Once each child determines his or her sign, the child will write at least three sentences about the characteristics for his or her sign on lined paper. Students will share their sentences with their peers in their group to make grammatical corrections before submitting the sentences to the teacher.
Closing: *Teacher responsible:* Both teachers	The teacher will tell students that a zodiac sign bar graph for the class has been created in the classroom. Each student will be given a piece of paper with his or her name on it. On their way out of class, they are to place their name in the appropriate zodiac sign category. The class will start the next day by looking at the results of the bar graph.
Homework: *Teacher responsible to assign:* Both teachers *Teacher responsible to correct:* Both teachers	Students will find the Chinese zodiac sign of at least three family members or friends.
Reflections:	

Figure 8–5. *(continued)*

planning time. Also, for the teacher playing the role of assistant, little curriculum knowledge is necessary. [...] Though, both teachers must be viewed by each other and by the students as equal contributors in the classroom. They must be seen as equal in behavior management, instruction, clerical duties, and more. If a co-teaching pair routinely implements one teach/one assist with the general education teacher acting as the lead, equality between the teachers will not be realized.

Co-teaching partners should use their common planning time to identify which of the five co-teaching models will be best suited for which lessons. It is recommended in the Co-Design Model to include a healthy diet of all five models. The particular model implemented should be determined according to student needs, curriculum knowledge of teachers, and if necessary, grouping decisions.

Students are placed in groups in the parallel, stations, and alternative models. Grouping decisions should be the responsibility of both teachers. Groups should be flexible and determined according to needs and abilities of students. Types of grouping include purposeful grouping and random grouping. Purposeful grouping simply means grouping students according to data and teacher input. This may include heterogeneous or homogeneous ability groupings, behavior groupings, or some combination of both.

The Role of the Paraprofessional in a Collaborative Environment

Friend (2005) states that co-teaching does not include the collaboration between a paraeducator and a professional. This is not to say that the role of the paraprofessional is insignificant. Quite the contrary. Paraprofessionals are integral to efforts to support and promote the education of all students. However, we caution educators to consider the proper use of the paraprofessional in the inclusive classroom. Bryant, Smith, and Bryant (2008) strongly recommend that teachers and paraeducators make clear the roles and responsibilities of each participant. This step ensures clarity of expectations for both the teacher and the paraprofessional.

Teachers are responsible for the actions of paraeducators who are under their supervision. Duties of the paraprofessional may include:

- Proctoring and grading exams
- Progress monitoring for behavior and academic success
- Reteaching or remediation of a topic
- Clerical duties
- Attendance at necessary meetings
- Attending to individual student needs (Bryant, Smith, & Bryant, 2008)

Barger-Anderson and et al. (2010) promote use of the paraeducator with teacher-planned activities for preteaching and for enrichment as well. Riggs (2005) cautions new teachers to be informed about the paraprofessional's background and experience but stresses the importance of recognizing the paraeducator as a worthy associate.

Blalock (1991) stresses the importance of proper training for paraprofessionals. We often provide for paraprofessional training within school districts. Training achieves the best results when conducted over several training sessions with topics generated by the school district. The Co-Design Model promotes paraprofessional training on topics such as collaboration, behavior management, and crisis prevention programs; their role and expectations in a collaborative classroom; and strategies and tactics to assist with remediation and practice of academic objectives.

Conclusion

It is important to note that successful co-teaching typically does not occur after a "one-shot" training session. Co-teaching tactics take time to develop via successful collaborative teacher interactions, training, and support. Collaborative co-teaching relationships should promote sharing of classroom duties. These aspects include establishing a common belief system for classroom management, common planning, accommodations and modifications for students with instruction, physical organization of the classroom, and accordance for assessments (Barger-Anderson et. al., 2010; Gately & Gately, 2001; Isherwood & Barger-Anderson, 2007). Zigmond and Magiera (2001) conclude that successful co-teaching results from careful planning, ongoing co-planning, enthusiastic pairs of teachers compatible in philosophy (as well as temperament and personality), and strong administrative support. Paraprofessionals can also be important partners in co-teaching approaches, if care is taken to delineate roles and provide appropriate training.

Murawski and Dieker (2004) imply that the method of co-teaching for collaborative instruction may increase learning outcomes for all students in the general education setting, while ensuring that students with disabilities receive necessary modifications and instruction by a content expert. Rice and Zigmond (2000) also conclude that well-implemented co-teaching could be beneficial for all students, both with and without disabilities.

Discussion Questions

These questions can be used as a basis for online discussion forums or as a starting point for discussion in the college classroom.

1. What are your own experiences with co-teaching? Did you enjoy the opportunity to have another teacher work with you in the classroom? Why or why not?

2. What are some creative ways you can come up with times to meet with a co-teacher within your present classroom schedule?

3. Choose one of the co-teaching models and develop an activity you might use in your own classroom that works well with this model.

4. Which model would you be the most uncomfortable trying out in your own classroom? Why?

5. Which co-teaching model have you already tried and found successful with your students? Why?

Figure Credits

Figures 8-1, 8-2, 8-3, 8-4, and 8-5: Copyright © 2013 by Keystone Educational Consulting Group. Reprinted with permission.

CHAPTER 9

Planning Instruction for Students with Significant Disabilities

Chapter Objectives

At the conclusion of the chapter, the reader will be able to:

- Respond to the questions of whether students with disabilities need and have access to the general education curriculum
- Identify effective ways to promote access to the general education curriculum for these students
- Determine effective strategies for teachers to use to successfully include students with significant disabilities in their classrooms

New Terminology

- Cognitive Disability
- Significant Disability
- Promoting Access

Introduction

This chapter looks at a small population of students that are increasingly included within the general education classroom. Within the chapter, the author responds to the questions: do students with disabilities need access to the general education curriculum, and do students with disabilities have access to the general education curriculum? Additionally, the topic of promoting access to the general education classroom and curriculum for these students is discussed. By the conclusion of the chapter, the reader will have new ideas on how to include students with greater needs into their own classroom successfully.

ACCESS TO GENERAL EDUCATION CURRICULUM FOR STUDENTS WITH SIGNIFICANT COGNITIVE DISABILITIES

Michael L. Wehmeyer

Credit: Michael L. Wehmeyer, "Access to General Education Curriculum for Students with Significant Cognitive Disabilities," *Handbook of Special Education*, pp. 544-556. Copyright © 2011 by Taylor & Francis Group. Reprinted with permission.

The 1997 amendments to the Individuals with Disabilities Education Act and their associated regulations included statutory and regulatory language intended to ensure that students with disabilities had "access" to the general curriculum. Section 300.347(a)(3) of that act required that the IEP of students with disabilities include:

> A statement of the special education and related services and supplementary aids and services to be provided to the child, or on behalf of the child, and a statement of the program modifications or supports for school personnel that will be provided for the child
> (i) to advance appropriately toward attaining the annual goals;
> (ii) to be involved and progress in the general curriculum;
> (iii) to be educated and participate with disabled and non-disabled children.

In fact, as reflected in the language in part (ii) above, what IDEA required was that students with disabilities be involved with and show progress in the general curriculum. The term "access to the general curriculum" refers to this requirement for student involvement and progress. The general curriculum was defined in the regulations as referring to "the same curriculum as for nondisabled children" (Federal Register, 1999, p. 12592). The intent of these access provisions was threefold, as described by U.S. Department of Education (U.S. Department of Education, 1995) officials: (1) that all students, including students with disabilities, would have access to a challenging curriculum; (2) that all students, including students with disabilities, would be held to high expectations; and (3) to align special education practice with accountability mechanisms emerging through school reform efforts.

The 2004 amendments to IDEA contained all of the original IDEA 1997 mandates and added several new requirements, including that schools ensure that the IEP (individual education program) team includes someone knowledgeable about the general education curriculum and that the team meet at least annually to address any lack of expected progress in the general education curriculum (these amendments also changed the term to "general education" curriculum). Finally, the regulations to IDEA 2004 (issued in June 2005) prohibited a student with a disability from being removed from the general education setting based solely upon needed modifications to the general education curriculum.

These "access to the general education curriculum" requirements were implemented to ensure that students with disabilities were not excluded from the accountability systems linked with standards-based reform inherent in the No Child Left Behind Act, which requires states to establish challenging academic content and student achievement standards that apply to all students, including students with severe disabilities. To that end, under NCLB, states may establish alternate achievement standards for students with the most significant cognitive disabilities. The act does not define "students with the most significant disabilities" explicitly, but instead caps "the number of proficient and advanced scores based on alternate achievement standards included in annual yearly progress (AYP) decisions" to "1.0 percent of the number of students enrolled in tested grades" (U.S. Department of Education, 2005). Thus, by default, students with the most significant cognitive disabilities refer to the lowest performing 1.0% of students in public schools. These students, in general, overlap with students who are receiving special education services under the categorical areas of intellectual disability, deaf-blindness, autism, and multiple disabilities, although it's important to note that the determination as to whether a student receives alternate assessments linked to the alternate achievement standards is an IEP team decision and not linked solely to disability labels, and not every student in these categorical areas will be eligible for alternate assessments.

The establishment of alternate standards is intended "to ensure that students with the most significant cognitive disabilities are fully included in State accountability systems and have access to challenging instruction linked to State content standards" (U.S. Department of Education, 2005). This intent is part of a general intent to align special education practices with standards-based reform efforts by (a) establishing high expectation that students with disabilities can meet the same standards as students without disabilities, (b) providing mechanisms to facilitate student involvement such as teacher qualifications, professional developmental and special programs and services, and (c) requiring reports on the results of assessments of student educational outcomes to monitor student progress (Lee, Wehmeyer, Soukup, & Palmer, 2010).

My purpose is to overview the state of the field with regard to promoting "access to the general education curriculum" for students with significant cognitive disabilities or, generally, students with the most severe disabilities. I examine whether students with severe disabilities have such access and the barriers to attaining said access, current strategies to promote access and standards-based learning, and the current evidence-base for this effort.

Do Students with Significant Cognitive Disabilities Need Access to the General Education Curriculum?

That students with severe disabilities are intended to be part of standards-based reform efforts was clearly expressed by both the IDEA access and alternate assessment mandates and the provision for alternate achievement standards in NCLB. That students with severe disabilities need to be included in such reforms or, more specifically, whether such students need access to the general education curriculum, is presumed by the establishment of such regulations and policies. As Browder, Wakeman, and Flowers (2006) noted, however, there is not universal agreement that the access mandates are either justified or warranted. Arguments in opposition of the inclusion of students with disabilities, and particularly students with severe disabilities, in standards-based reform include that such efforts overlook previous experiences of failure within the general education curriculum by students with disabilities; concerns about the loss of individualization in the education of students with disabilities; concerns about the potential of increased dropout of students with disabilities; concerns about the minimization of functional or related content, including a focus on transition-related activities for adolescents with disabilities; and perceptions that content-focused instruction is not appropriate or viable for students with more severe disabilities.

As illustration of the latter, Agran, Alper, and Wehmeyer (2002) conducted a survey of teachers working with students with severe disabilities about their perception of the access requirements and their students. A high proportion (81%) indicated that their students were included in general education classrooms at least a portion of the school day. When asked if ensuring students' access to the general curriculum would help *increase educational expectations* for students with disabilities, 75% of teachers agreed to some degree. Sixty-three percent, however, indicated that they felt access to the general education curriculum was *more* important for students with high-incidence disabilities.

These concerns about the involvement of students with disabilities in standards-based reform have been countered with suggestions of the potential benefit of such involvement. Among these are the potential for higher levels of learning as a result of higher quality instruction; higher expectations for student progress; opportunities to learn content that had previously been ignored; greater inclusion in the general education classroom; and greater accountability for ensuring that students with disabilities actually learn (Browder, Wakeman, et al., 2006).

Of particular concern has been the involvement of students with disabilities in high-stakes or statewide testing. While concerns with regard to students with more severe disabilities and high stakes testing warrants discussion, the research suggests that for many students with higher incidence disabilities, the benefits of inclusion in standards-based reform seem to outweigh the risks if those risks are taken into account and their negative consequences mitigated. Ysseldyke, Dennison, and Nelson (2003) reported the positive consequences of the involvement of students with disabilities being involved in large-scale assessment and accountability systems as including higher expectations and standards for students with disabilities, improved instruction, improved student performance, increased general and special education collaboration, and increased communication with parents. Whether these same benefits accrue to students with severe disabilities remains to be established, though as research to be highlighted later in this chapter suggests, there is already evidence that inclusion in standards-based learning has the benefit of promoting student involvement in the general education classroom and of emphasizing the need for specific curriculum modifications and, thus, higher quality instruction in general education settings.

Although this chapter will not focus extensively on issues pertaining to alternate assessment, it is relevant to note that many of the concerns relative to other student populations with regard to statewide testing are not relevant to the discussion of the application of standards based learning for students with severe disabilities. Of course, statewide or large-scale testing is the mechanism used in NCLB to determine student AYP and to determine which students need additional instruction. Students with the most severe disabilities, however, are exempted from the statewide test if deemed appropriate by the IEP team, and become eligible for assessment using an alternate assessment. The U.S. Department of Education (2005) defined alternate assessment as "an assessment designed for the small number of students with disabilities who are unable to participate in the regular state assessment even with appropriate accommodations" (p. 797). Importantly, such alternate assessments must be aligned with the state's content standards, through the use of alternate student performance standards, and must be implemented in a manner that supports the use of results from such assessments to determine AYP for this population. As such, the alternate assessment process is designed to provide reliable and valid assessments of the progress of students with severe disabilities and to contribute to decisions about AYP and resource allocation.

Further, it is also important to point out that the IDEA regulations do not require that the educational programs of students with severe disabilities be determined exclusively by the general education curriculum. Indeed, these regulations stipulate that the educational programs of students with disabilities should include a focus on the general education curriculum *to the maximum degree appropriate*. IDEA continues to require that the educational programs of students with disabilities address "other educational needs" that are not part of the general education curriculum. While IDEA's prohibition against excluding students from the general education classroom based solely on needed modifications to the general education curriculum and the act's requirement that students not be removed from the general education classroom unless supplementary aids and services and specially designed instruction have been provided and deemed unsuccessful seems to make the omission of all general education curriculum content from a student's educational program inadvisable, the act also clearly expects students to receive instruction to promote both academic achievement and enhanced functional performance. Again, the determination of what proportion of the student's educational program reflects instruction derived from the general education curriculum versus functional content is an IEP team decision, and factors such as age, grade level, and severity of disability will all factor into that decision.

Whether students with severe disabilities can benefit from instruction in core content areas, opinions and perceptions aside, is essentially still an open question. As part of an OSEP-funded project to review the literature in core content instruction for students with severe disabilities, Browder, Spooner, Wakeman, Trela, and Baker (2006) summarized a number of studies synthesizing the "research-based evidence on whether this population can learn academics" (p. 311). In the area of reading, Browder and colleagues found strong evidence for teaching sight words (comprehension) to students with severe disabilities, but inadequate consideration of other components of reading instruction (phonemic awareness, phonics, fluency, and vocabulary).

In math, Browder, Spooner, and colleagues (2006) found evidence for the efficacy of teaching math measurement skills using systematic prompting and massed trial instruction, but again inadequate consideration of instruction in other components of math instruction, including number and operations, data analysis and probability, geometry, and algebra. Butler, Miller, Lee, and Pierce (2001) also reviewed the literature pertaining to teaching mathematics to students with intellectual disability with mild/moderate impairments, finding that students benefited from "interventions stressing frequent feedback, explicit instruction, and ample drill and practice" (p. 29), though also found preliminary results from studies on teaching multi-step, higher-level computation and problem-solving for students with intellectual disability to be encouraging.

In the area of science, Courtade, Spooner, and Browder (2006) found only 11 studies in a 20-year span focused on science instruction for students with severe disabilities, most of which focused on skills that these authors referred to as falling in the "Personal and Social Perspectives" content area, which encompassed issues such as safety, injury prevention, nutrition, or health.

It is important, as such, not to overstate the case for an evidence-base for teaching core content areas to students with severe disabilities. There is some evidence that students with severe disabilities can learn basic reading, math, and science knowledge and skills, but that research has been conducted primarily within a functional/life skills curricular paradigm and fails to address key components of effective instruction across content areas. Further, the low-incidence nature of severe disabilities leads to a preponderance of single-subject and quasi-experimental design studies and there are not sufficient large-scale, randomized trial studies documenting the efficacy (or lack thereof) of instruction to promote such outcomes. It is equally important, however, to emphasize that there is *not* an evidence-base suggesting that if provided high quality instruction (particularly, as discussed subsequently, embodying strategies incorporating Universal Design for Learning) students will *not* benefit. Put another way, what is most evident from the extant literature base is that there has been virtually no research on the effects of instruction to promote critical components of reading such as phonemic awareness or fluency; components of math instruction such as number and operations and geometry; or virtually any component of science instruction or research outside the functional or life skills mind-set that has dominated instructional models for this population.

There has, though, been progress in research pertaining to content instruction for students with severe disabilities since the Browder, Wakeman, et al. (2006) review. For example, Jimenez, Browder, and Courtade (2008) examined the effect of systematic instruction with concrete representation on the acquisition of an algebra skill for students with moderate developmental disabilities. This multiple-probe-across-participants design study found that students were able to learn how to solve an algebraic equation, including a demonstration of their capacity to generalize this skill across materials and settings. Browder, Ahlgrim-Delzell, Courtade,

Gibbs, and Flowers (2008) provided evidence of the efficacy of an early literacy intervention for students with significant developmental disabilities using a randomized control group design study. Students in the treatment group made significant gains on multiple measures of readings skills, including measures of phonemic awareness. Similarly, Browder, Mims, Spooner, Ahlgram-Delzell, and Lee (2008) showed that young students with severe disabilities could improve literacy skills by engaging in shared reading of a story. Konrad, Trela, and Test (2006) evaluated the efficacy of a self-regulated writing strategy with high school students with multiple disabilities and showed positive effects on paragraph writing skills. Collins, Evans, Creech-Galloway, Karl, and Miller (2007) showed that students with severe disabilities could acquire both functional and core content sight words in general education classrooms using either direct distributed trial instruction or embedded distributed trial instruction. Browder, Trela, and Jimenez (2007) showed the efficacy of using task analysis to teach a story-based literacy lesson using adapted, grade-appropriate middle school literature to students with moderate and severe developmental disabilities.

An additional argument for focusing on the general education curriculum for students with severe disabilities is the fact that, as noted by Wehmeyer, Field, Doren, Jones, and Mason (2004), there is considerable overlap between the general education curriculum (as defined by content and student achievement standards) and some important traditional "special education" instructional areas. For example, most state and local content and student achievement standards across multiple content areas contain language pertaining to component elements of self-determined behavior, such as goal setting, problem solving, and decision making, the promotion of which is an important component of the educational programs of many students with disabilities and potentially as important for all students.

In fact, in a content analysis of the curricular philosophies reflected in states' alternate assessment performance indicators, Browder et al. (2004) concluded that the influence of a "functional curriculum philosophy," reflecting a curricular focus on functional and life skills instruction, was still evident in most such standards. Similarly, Browder et al. (2004) examined the actual alternate assessment content for alternate assessments for 31 states and concluded that while there was a strong focus on academic skills, the assessments also reflect "an additive curriculum approach to linking academic and functional skills" (p. 211). In other words, the general education curriculum as currently defined for students with more severe disabilities (incorporating alternate achievement standards) provides ample room to address the functional and life skills important for students within this population.

Ultimately, as such, if there are concerns about the undue or unintended consequences of involving students with severe disabilities in the general education curriculum, the provisions in NCLB and IDEA pertaining to alternate assessments and alternate achievement standards, the IDEA requirement that the other educational needs of students with disabilities continue to be addressed, and the fact that the general education curriculum does contain content that is important to students with severe disabilities would seem to mitigate against, at the very least, the exclusion of students with severe disabilities from such reform efforts. Further, of course, there is no ambiguity in the federal legislation pertaining to such access and student involvement in assessments. All students must be included in state assessments and all students with disabilities must be provided an educational program that ensures involvement with and progress in the general education classroom.

Do Students with Significant Cognitive Disabilities Have Access to the General Education Curriculum?

To address the evidence-base that would lead us to a conclusion with regard to whether students with severe disabilities have access to the general education curriculum, one must examine several sources, beginning with teacher survey data. The aforementioned survey of teachers of students with severe disabilities pertaining to access issues (Agran et al., 2002) found that while between 11% and 23% of respondents indicated they used several different ways to ensure some level of access, the largest proportion (37%) indicated that students were receiving an educational program developed wholly outside the context of the general curriculum. A little over one-third of teachers indicated they were frequently involved in curriculum planning meetings with general educators. Most teachers identified a paraprofessional as the primary means of supporting students in the general curriculum, with one-third indicating that materials were adapted for use by students with severe disabilities. Nearly three-fourths of respondents indicated that students with disabilities were evaluated exclusively by criteria stipulated in the IEP.

Dymond, Renzaglia, Gilson, and Slagor (2007) interviewed teachers working with students with and without disabilities to determine how they perceived or understood what was meant by "access to the general education curriculum" as it might apply to students with significant cognitive disabilities. A high proportion (80%) of respondents discussed core content issues in responding to queries with regard to what they interpreted access to the general education curriculum to mean, though only half of general educators and 9% of special educators actually defined it as does IDEA (e.g., access to the same curriculum as all other students). Further, general education teachers most frequently defined access for students with significant disabilities as instruction in core content areas in the general education classroom using the same curriculum and materials provided to students without disabilities. Special educators, however, defined it as having access to an adapted curriculum that was "relevant and meaningful to the student and addresses individual student needs and interests" (p. 11).

The absence of goals related to core content areas in the IEPs of students with severe disabilities, despite IDEA mandates and research supporting such a focus, has been documented and forms a second level of evidence with regard to student access to the general education curriculum. Karvonen and Huynh (2007) examined the relationship between curricular priorities reflected in a student's IEP and content and performance expectations in the alternate assessment. Specifically, Karvonen and Huynh (2007) examined IEPs in relation to alternate achievement standards and alternate assessment pertaining to language arts and math. There were few IEP goals related to either objective, though slightly more related to language arts, but those objectives that did exist were consistent with the functional paradigm discussed previously (e.g., math measurement objectives such as telling time, using a calendar, as opposed to other components).

There are also several studies examining more directly the degree to which students with more severe disabilities have such access. Roach and Elliott (2006) conducted a study examining the influence of the access to the general education curriculum of students with significant cognitive disabilities, as measured by a teacher questionnaire, on the performance of these students on a state alternate assessment in reading, language arts, and math. Using structural equation modeling, Roach and Elliott found that students who had greater access to the general education curriculum, increased time in the general education classroom, and academic goals on their IEP performed better on the reading, language arts, and math assessments.

Wehmeyer, Lattin, Lapp-Rincker, and Agran (2003) conducted an observational study of 33 students with intellectual disability to examine the degree to which they were involved in tasks related to the general education curriculum. Students were observed in naturally occurring classroom contexts from 120 to 240 minutes each, with an average of 202 minutes per student. Overall, almost 110 hours of observations were coded, and students were observed to be engaged in a task related to a school district standard, either working on the same task as peers or a task related to a different standard or benchmark in 70% of intervals. This varied considerably by student level of disability, though, with students with limited support needs (mild disabilities) engaged in a task linked to a standard on 87% of intervals, and students with significant cognitive disabilities doing so 55% of the time. Students served in the general education classroom were observed working on tasks linked to a standard 90% of intervals, while students served primarily in self-contained settings engaged in tasks related to a standard in only 50% of the observations intervals.

Overall, students with intellectual disability were working on a task linked to an IEP 22% of the intervals, were provided accommodations to work on a task linked to a standard 5% of the time, were working on an adapted task 3% of the time, and were being taught strategies to improve their capacity to engage with the general curriculum only 0.15% of the time. Moreover, there were significant differences by setting (inclusive or self-contained) in a number of areas. Students served in inclusive settings were significantly more likely to be working on a task linked to a standard and to be working on an adapted task. Students educated primarily in self-contained settings were significantly more likely to be working on a task linked to a standard below grade level or on a task not linked to a standard, and to be working on a task linked to an IEP objective.

In a second study using a computer-based data collection system, Soukup, Wehmeyer, Bashinski, and Bovaird (2007) examined the degree to which 19 late elementary age students with intellectual disability had access to activities that could be linked to district standards in social studies and science. In 61% of intervals (n = 3,420 20-second intervals), students' activities could be linked to a grade level standard, and in an additional 20% of intervals could be linked to an off-grade level standard. However, when examined based on how much time the student spent in the general education classroom, 83% of intervals for students in a high inclusion group and 93% of intervals for students in a moderate inclusion group could be linked to grade level standards, while none of the intervals for students in the low inclusion group (e.g., self-contained classroom) were linked to grade-level standards (groups did not differ by level of impairment). In only 18% of the intervals was a curriculum adaptation in place to support a student, and there was no instance in which students were being taught learning-to-learn strategies and other strategies to enable them to interact with content.

Lee, Wehmeyer, Palmer, Soukup, and Little (2008) used the same computer-based recording system in a study to examine the impact of promoting self-determination on student access to the general education, and in baseline data collection involving nearly 90 hours of observations determined similar trends for 45 high school students with intellectual or developmental disabilities. These observations occurred exclusively in the general education classroom, and on almost 80% of intervals students with disabilities were working on grade-level standards (compared to 93% of the time for peers without disabilities). Further, in another 18% of intervals students with disabilities were working on an off-grade level standard. This instruction matched poorly with IEP goal instruction, as on only 26% of the intervals was an IEP goal addressed, validating the aforementioned lack of alignment between IEP goals and the access mandates. Also, during only 24% of the intervals in which a student was observed to be working on a grade-level standard were any level of adaptations documented.

Similarly, Matzen, Ryndak, and Nakao (in press) conducted structured interviews and classroom observations comparing instructional activities for students with significant cognitive disabilities in both general education and self-contained classrooms, and found that when in general education contexts, students were disproportionately exposed to grade level academic content, while during instruction in self-contained settings they were not.

In summary, the existing evidence suggests that the degree to which students with severe disabilities have access to the general education curriculum is, in large measure, a function of context. Students receiving their education in self-contained settings tend to work on IEP goals that, in general, tend not to be focused on the general education classroom or on off-grade standards. Students educated in the general education classroom, however, have frequent opportunities to work on tasks linked to grade-level standards. This finding is consistent with studies showing that students with disabilities make greater progress when provided core content instruction in the general education classroom. Cole, Waldron, and Majd (2004), for example, explored student progress on reading and math assessments for students with disabilities in general education and self-contained classrooms, and found that students with disabilities receiving core content instruction in the general education classroom made comparable or greater than average academic progress when compared with students without disabilities in the same classes, a finding not repeated for students receiving core content instruction in self-contained settings.

That said, it is also clear that too few students receiving instruction in core content areas in the general education classroom had access to modified curricular materials and accommodations that would address issues of progress. The absence of such modifications is a critical factor in ensuring progress and not just access. Lee et al. (2010) studied whether curriculum modifications predicted adaptive or maladaptive student behaviors in general education settings for students with developmental disabilities and determined when students were engaged in tasks linked to an on- or off-grade standard without the support of any curriculum modification, they were more likely to be engaged in behaviors that competed with active engagement, but when engaged with standards and provided any type of curriculum modifications, were disproportionately likely to be engaged in academically beneficial responses.

Finally, it was clear that teachers, particularly teachers working with students with severe disabilities, hold paradoxical 'opinions about issues of access to the general education curriculum, recognizing that efforts to promote such access would raise expectations but in general believing that a focus on access was more relevant to other students with less intensive support needs, and defining access, as it were, as access to a modified, adapted curriculum that was more functional in nature.

Promoting Access to the General Education Curriculum for Students with Significant Cognitive Disabilities

A number of frameworks to promote access to the general education curriculum for students with more severe disabilities have been proposed (Browder & Spooner, 2006; Janney & Snell, 2004; Jorgensen, McSheehan, & Sonnenmeier, 2010; McSheehan, Sonnenmeier, Jorgensen, & Turner, 2006; Spooner, Dymond, Smith, & Kennedy, 2006; Wehmeyer, Lance, & Bashinski, 2002; Wehmeyer, Sands, Knowlton, & Kozleski, 2002). Rather than describe each of these independently, the following section is structured by the types of actions that can be taken at district, campus, and classroom levels that are necessary to implement standards-based learning for students with severe disabilities, and key elements of the above listed models will be incorporated into these sections.

DISTRICT LEVEL ACTIONS TO PROMOTE ACCESS TO THE GENERAL EDUCATION CLASSROOM FOR STUDENTS WITH SIGNIFICANT COGNITIVE DISABILITIES

Standards setting. School reform efforts in the era of NCLB begin with and are centered on the establishment of standards that define the curriculum for all students and become the basis for accountability assessment procedures. No Child Left Behind (2002) requires that states establish "challenging academic content and student academic achievement standards that will be used by the State, its local educational agencies (LEAs), and its schools" [Sec. 200.1(a)]. Two aspects of the standards setting process seem particularly important to promote access for all students, including students with severe disabilities. First, standards should be set across a broad array of content areas if the general curriculum is to be appropriate for all students. Currently, NCLB requires standards only for a limited set of academic content areas and many content areas important to students with significant cognitive disabilities, including functional or life skills content or transition content, are not well integrated into the standards and, consequently, into the curriculum. That said, as noted previously, the alternate student performance standards set for use in alternate assessment tend to reflect an emphasis on life skills and functional content.

Second, if students with widely varying skills, backgrounds, knowledge, and customs are to progress in the general curriculum, the standards upon which the curriculum is based, as well as the curriculum itself, must embody the principles of universal design (discussed subsequently), and be written to be open-ended and inclusive, not close-ended and exclusive. The terms "open- and close-ended" refer to "the amount of specificity and direction provided by curriculum standards, benchmarks, goals, or objectives at both the building and classroom levels" (Wehmeyer et al., 2002, p. 126). Close-ended standards are specific and require narrowly defined outcomes or performance indicators, like "writing a five-page paper on the cause of the Civil War" (Wehmeyer et al., 2002, p. 126). Open-ended standards do not restrict the ways in which students exhibit knowledge or skills and focus more on the expectations that students will interact with the content, ask questions, manipulate materials, make observations, and then communicate their knowledge in a variety of ways (orally, through video tape, writing and directing a play, etc.). Open-ended designs allow for greater flexibility as to what, when, and how topics will be addressed in the classroom (Stainback, Stainback, Stefanich, & Alper, 1996) and are more consistent with universally designed curriculum, ensuring that more students, including students with intellectual disability, can show progress in the curriculum (Wehmeyer et al., 2002).

Curriculum alignment. The alignment of the curriculum with these standards is the next step in standards-based learning, though for students with severe disabilities this alignment process involves multiple steps beyond the alignment of the content standards and student performance standards with the curriculum, to include an alignment between alternate achievement standards with content standards and the general education curriculum, and between IEP goals and the general education curriculum. Although no national study has been conducted examining the alignment of IEP goals to content standards, the studies by Karvonen and Huynh (2007), Wehmeyer, Lattin, et al. (2003), and Soukup et al. (2007) discussed previously provide indirect evidence of the lack of alignment between IEP goals and content standards and/or the general education curriculum.

Browder et al. (2004) examined the alternate assessments from 31 states to determine the alignment between performance indicators for students with severe disabilities and national standards in math and language arts. Of the 31 states, only the performance indicators of three states were determined to be in alignment with math and language arts standards set by national organizations specializing in those areas. Of course, the alignment between alternate achievement standards and national standards is not necessarily the same as alignment between alternate achievement standards and state content standards, but nevertheless it seems evident that more progress needs to be made in aligning alternate achievement standards and alternate assessments to content standards established for all students.

CAMPUS AND BUILDING LEVEL ACTIONS TO PROMOTE ACCESS TO THE GENERAL EDUCATION CURRICULUM FOR STUDENTS WITH SIGNIFICANT COGNITIVE DISABILITIES

Several whole school or schoolwide actions support greater access for students with severe disabilities. Whole school interventions are, quite simply, those implemented throughout the school campus and with all students. Such interventions have the effect of minimizing the need for more individualized interventions and, in turn, foster a climate in which students with severe disabilities can benefit from instruction in the general education classroom and curriculum.

Curriculum mapping　Many schools use a curriculum mapping process—which involves the collection of information about each teacher's curriculum, including descriptions of the content to be taught during the year, processes and skills emphasized, and student assessments used, using the school calendar as an organizer—to find gaps or repetition in the curriculum content and to be sure they are teaching all parts of the curriculum framework, performance objectives, and other standards at the appropriate grade/course. These curriculum maps can, in turn, be used to identify where in the curriculum and across the school day students with significant cognitive disabilities can receive instruction on content from the general curriculum that is based on the student's unique learning needs.

Universal Design for Learning　An important component of most models to promote student access involves the application of principles of Universal Design for Learning (UDL) in the education of all students. Orkwis and McLane (1998) defined "universal design for learning" as "the design of instructional materials and activities that allows the learning goals to be achievable by individuals with wide differences in their abilities to see, hear, speak, move, read, write, understand English, attend, organize, engage, and remember" (p. 9). The onus is on curriculum planners and designers to employ principles of universal design to ensure that students with a wide range of capacities can access, advance, and succeed in the curriculum.

Researchers at the Center for Applied Special Technology (CAST, 1998–1999) suggested three essential *qualities* of UDL. These qualities are that the curriculum is designed to (a) provide *multiple representations* of content, (b) provide *multiple options for expression* and control, and (c) provide *multiple options for engagement* and motivation. These are described below.

- *Curriculum provides multiple means of representation.* Researchers at CAST suggested that "universally designed materials accommodate diversity through alternative representations of key information. Students with different preferences and needs can either select the representational medium most suitable for them, or gather information from a variety of representational media simultaneously." World Wide Web pages designed to be accessible present an example of using multiple means of representation. One of the benefits of the WWW is the capacity to use graphic images in a variety of ways, from icons to hyperlinked pictures and streamed video. However, for a person who is blind or visually impaired using a text-reader to access the site, graphic depictions may make the site and the information contained therein inaccessible. As an alternative, accessible web sites include text descriptions of images and pictures. Similarly, the design of curricular materials should include multiple representations of important topics, features, or points. Such representations include a variety of methods of presentation of the material based on learner needs and characteristics. Students with significant cognitive disabilities, for example, need print information to be presented with graphic depictions, free from unnecessary clutter and with key information repeated or highlighted.

- *Curriculum provides multiple means of expression.* CAST researchers noted that the dominant means of expression used in schools has been written. However, there are a variety of ways of student responding that could indicate progress, including "artwork, photography, drama, music, animation, and video," (CAST, 1998–1999) that would enable students to express their ideas and their knowledge.

- *Curriculum provides multiple means of engagement.* Student engagement in learning has long been an indicator of motivation in the classroom. By the utilization of multiple representation and presentation modes, particularly those that involve digital representation of knowledge which are graphically-based and incorporate video, audio and other multimedia components, student engagement, and as such student motivation, can be enhanced. Universally designed curriculum takes into account individual student interests and preferences and individualizes representation, presentation, and response aspects of the curriculum delivery accordingly. Current technologies allow that level of individualization and, thus, provide greater flexibility in ways for the student to engage in learning. (CAST, 1998–1999)

Research evidence documenting the effects of UDL on access to or progress in the general education curriculum for students with disabilities is limited. Kortering, McLannon, and Braziel (2008) found that students with high incidence disabilities perceived instruction in algebra and biology with universally designed materials to be more engaging than traditional instruction. Spooner, Baker, Harris, Ahlgrim-Delzell, and Browder (2007) found that training teachers to apply principles of UDL to their classroom context resulted in significant changes to lesson planning by this group, with lessons incorporating principles of UDL post-training. Dymond et al. (2006) documented the efficacy of infusing UDL into a Science class on student engagement with Science content.

Obviously, there is a need for research examining the effect of UDL on standards-based learning for students with severe disabilities.

Instructional context   Put simply, the limited evidence that exists at this time suggests strongly that the place a student receives instruction in the general education curriculum is the general education classroom. Studies highlighted previously (Cole et al., 2004; Lee et al., 2008; Matzen et al., in press; Soukup et al., 2007; Wehmeyer, Lattin, et al., 2003) all provided evidence that students with severe disabilities had greater access to the general education curriculum and were disproportionately more likely to be working on tasks linked to a grade-level core-content standard when they were receiving instruction in the general education classroom.

Instructional strategies   It goes without saying that high quality instruction with regard to core-academic content is critical to the success of all students, including students with severe disabilities. [...] We will only note that access to and progress in the general education curriculum for students with severe disabilities is obviously contingent on schoolwide implementation of high quality instructional strategies. Spooner et al. (2006) identified a few approaches to promoting the access of students with severe disabilities that illustrate the types of instructional strategies that should or could promote access and progress. One such set of instructional strategies involves peer support interventions, in which "peers are taught to provide support by adapting class activities to facilitate student participation" (p. 278). Carter and colleagues (Carter, Cushing, Clark, and Kennedy, 2005; Carter & Kennedy, 2006; Carter, Sisco, Melekoglu, & Kurkowski, 2007) have examined the utilization of peer support interventions to promote access to the general education and social interactions for students with severe disabilities, particularly as an alternative to the use of paraprofessionals in instructional support roles. These studies have documented that students with severe disabilities supported by peers "showed substantially higher levels of active engagement relative to receiving supports from paraprofessionals and special educators" (Spooner et al., p. 286) and that students had higher levels of social interactions and contact with the general education curriculum when students worked with two peers relative to one peer.

Another instructional approach identified by Spooner et al. (2006) involves instruction to promote self-determination. Wehmeyer et al. (2004) noted that efforts to promote self-determination may be beneficial to gaining access to the general education for two reasons; first, most district standards, particularly student achievement standards, include component elements of instruction to promote self-determination, such as goal setting, problem solving or decision making, as elements of the standard. As such, promoting self-determination, which involves instruction in areas such as these, provides an entry point for gaining access to the general education curriculum for students with severe disabilities and provides a focal point for classroom-wide instruction. Second, it is hypothesized that students who are more self-determined will, in fact, perform more effectively in the general education curriculum. There is a clear evidence-base that teaching students to self-regulate learning or teaching students self-directed learning strategies such as self-monitoring or self-instruction has beneficial outcomes for students with severe disabilities in student goal attainment, problem solving, and student engagement (Agran, Blanchard, Hughes, & Wehmeyer, 2002; Agran et al., 2005; Hughes et al., 2002). Further, the application of instruction to teach and implement these strategies has been validated as effective in promoting standards-based learning for students with severe disabilities (Wehmeyer, Hughes, et al., 2003). Finally, Wehmeyer and colleagues have provided evidence that teaching students to self-regulate learning using the Self-Determined Learning Model of Instruction (Wehmeyer, Palmer, Agran, Mithaug, & Martin, 2000) results in the attainment of goals linked to the general education curriculum (Agran, Wehmeyer, Cavin, & Palmer, in press; Lee et al., 2010; Palmer, Wehmeyer, Gipson, & Agran, 2004).

Teacher training It is self-evident that high quality instruction and teacher training are causally linked, and similarly self-evident that a critical schoolwide component of efforts to promote access to and progress in the general education curriculum for students with severe disabilities will involve teacher training. As noted previously, Spooner et al. (2007), training in UDL, improved the lesson plans of teachers working with students with severe disabilities. Clark, Cushing, and Kennedy (2004) documented the efficacy of an intensive onsite technical assistance model for special educators as resulting in greater access to the general education curriculum for students with severe disabilities. Dymond and colleagues (2006) indicated the importance and efficacy of team collaboration and planning in infusing UDL into a science course for students with severe disabilities, and Jorgensen and colleagues (McSheehan et al.,

2006; Sonnenmeir, McSheehan, & Jorgensen, 2005) have demonstrated the efficacy of a team planning process to implement a model to promote student progress in the general education curriculum (Beyond Access Model) with students with severe disabilities who need augmentative communication supports. The Beyond Access Model creates Comprehensive Assessment of Student and Team Supports (CASTS) process to gain information from team members as a means of implementing the model and promoting student progress in core content areas. Activities that occur during this time include (beyond standard team activities pertaining to special education practices) identifying the alignment between the student's educational program and best practices for learning core content in the general education classroom and alignment of staffing and teaming practices to achieve progress.

CURRICULUM PLANNING AND EDUCATIONAL DECISION MAKING TO PROMOTE ACCESS TO THE GENERAL EDUCATION CURRICULUM FOR STUDENTS WITH SIGNIFICANT COGNITIVE DISABILITIES

From the school level, the obvious next level of action involves the educational decision-making process that determines the educational programs of students with disabilities. That is, obviously, the IEP process for students with severe disabilities. To a large degree, a focus on access to the general education curriculum for students with severe disabilities changes the role of the IEP in the design of a student's educational program. Historically, the IEPs of many students with severe disabilities described an *alternative* curriculum focused solely on life skills outcomes and functional content. The access mandates in IDEA, though, presume that the general education curriculum is the starting point for educational program decision making and require IEP teams to consider curricular modifications, supplementary aids and services, specially designed instruction, and related services that promote access and progress. The IEP is not intended to describe an alternative curriculum; instead, it is intended to identify the supports a student needs to be involved with and progress in the general education curriculum and, only then, what other educational needs are not addressed in the general education classroom that warrant instructional focus. As stated by Nolet and McLaughlin (2000), the IEP should be a plan to identify goals and objectives needed to enhance, not replace, the general education curriculum.

Wehmeyer, Lattin, et al. (2003) proposed a model for use by IEP teams to design IEPs that are consistent with the intent of the access mandates (see Figure 9.1). As shown in this figure, the decision-making process begins with the general education curriculum and knowledge (from assessment, stakeholder input, and prior instructional experiences) about the unique

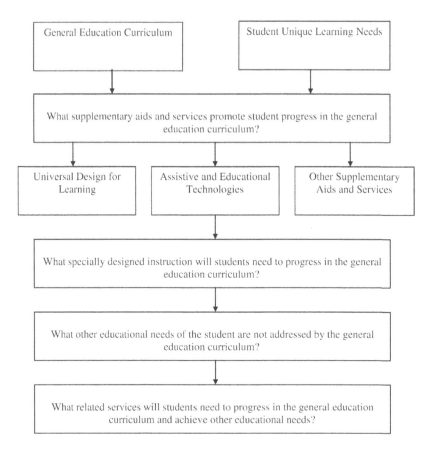

Figure 9-1. IEP Team decision making process to promote access to the general education curriculum.

learning needs of the student (e.g., functional/life skills needs). Next, as per the IDEA requirements, the IEP team has a number of responsibilities when writing the IEP. They must:

- Develop measurable goals to ensure student progress in the general education curriculum and to address other educational needs that are not in the general education curriculum.
- Identify the specially designed instruction required to ensure student progress in the general education curriculum.

- Identify the supplementary aids and services required to ensure that students can be educated with their non-disabled peers and make progress in the general education curriculum.
- Identify related services students need if they are reasonably to be expected to benefit from the educational program.
- Determine if a student can participate in the state mandated tests without modifications or if the student requires a modified test or an alternative assessment.

Teams are guided through this process by asking and answering four questions:

1. What supplementary aids and services promote student progress in the general education curriculum?

2. What specially designed instruction will students need to progress in the general education curriculum?

3. What other educational needs of the student are not addressed by the general education curriculum?

4. What related services will students need to progress in the general education curriculum and achieve other educational needs?

IDEA defines supplementary aids and services as "aids, services, and other supports that are provided in general education classes or other education related settings to enable children with disabilities to be educated with non-disabled children to the maximum extent appropriate" (2004, section §300.320(a)(4)). Such supplementary aids and supports include modifications to the curriculum or the classroom (room or seating arrangement), extended time to complete tasks, extended school year services, assistive technology devices, a paraprofessional or notetaker, and other accommodations to promote regular classroom participation. Issues pertaining to UDL come into play here, with IEP teams considering how to modify the presentation or representation of content information or student's responses to the content (discussed previously) to promote student access and progress.

Wehmeyer, Hughes, et al. (2003) have suggested two levels of curriculum modifications as important in the education of students with significant cognitive disabilities: adapting the curriculum and augmenting the curriculum. The first level of modification involves curriculum adaptations. Curriculum adaptation refers to the application of principles of UDL to modify the way the curriculum looks (representation), is presented (presentation), or the ways in which students respond or engage with the curriculum. Adaptations to the way curricular content is *represented* refer to the way in which the information in the curriculum is depicted or portrayed, specifically how curricular materials are used to depict information. As noted, the dominant representation mode in education involves print materials, usually through texts, workbooks, and worksheets. Curriculum adaptations modify that representation so a wider array of students can progress, ranging from changing font size to using graphics to using technology and electronic text.

Adaptations in curriculum *presentation* modify the way teachers convey or impart information in the content in curriculum. Such presentation has, historically, been through written formats (chalkboards or overheads) or verbally (lectures). These primary means of presentation have drawbacks for many students who read ineffectively (or don't read at all) or who have difficulty attending to or understanding lecture formats. There are a variety of ways of changing the presentation mode, from using video sources, to reading (or playing an audiotape of) written materials to web-based information.

Curriculum adaptations that modify the student's *engagement* with the curriculum impact the ways students respond to the curriculum. Again, the typical means of student engagement within the curriculum involves written responses or, perhaps less frequently, oral responses or reports. There are, however, a variety of ways in which students can respond to content beyond a written report, from multi-media presentations like PowerPoint or through video, to performance-based expressions and artistic products.

The second level of curricular modification to achieve access involves curriculum *augmentation* (Wehmeyer, Hughes, et al., 2003). Curriculum augmentations refer to the expansion of the general education curriculum to include content that teaches students learning to learn, cognitive, or self-management strategies to enable them to interact more effectively with the general curriculum. Such augmentations don't change the curriculum, but add to or augment the curriculum with strategies for students to succeed within the curriculum. The aforementioned focus on promoting self-determination and student-directed learning is a means of curriculum augmentation. Teaching students such strategies allows them to manage, direct, and regulate their own learning, and permits students to plan, execute, and evaluate actions based on problem solving and self-directed decision making (Agran, King-Sears, Wehmeyer, & Copeland, 2003).

IDEA defines "special education" as "specially designed instruction." In addition to the schoolwide implementation of high quality instruction, students with significant cognitive disabilities will undoubtedly need additional instructional supports.

Only after teams have considered supplementary aids and services and specially designed instruction that would enable students to engage with the general education curriculum should they then consider what unique student learning needs are not addressed in the general education curriculum and, finally, what related services are needed to enable students to be involved with and progress in the general education curriculum or achieve goals related to other educational needs.

CLASSROOM LEVEL ACTIONS TO PROMOTE ACCESS TO THE GENERAL EDUCATION CURRICULUM FOR STUDENTS WITH SIGNIFICANT COGNITIVE DISABILITIES

Designing units of study   Units of study are the "maps" that teachers create to organize and plan for how they are going to support students to learn and demonstrate their understanding of the content, skills, processes, and knowledge required to achieve grade-level and broader school outcomes. Broadly, unit planning models tend to be organized by subject area, discipline structure, integrated designs, learner-centered designs, experience-centered designs, problem centered designs, and life-situations designs (Wehmeyer et al., 2002). Such units of study identify what needs to be accomplished by the end of the school year, district standards and benchmarks, and student knowledge and instructional needs. Once teachers understand the "big picture" for the school year, they must "backwards-map" to determine what students will need to know and do by the middle of the year, and then plan for more manageable instructional units. When a teacher has an overall idea of what needs to be accomplished by the end of the school year and has "chunked" that content, skills, and knowledge into mid-year and quarterly components, he/she is ready to plan units of instruction (Wehmeyer, Sands, et al., 2002).

It is at the unit planning level that teachers must identify the "big ideas" they want to achieve in each unit. The big ideas are those concepts, knowledge, and skills that a teacher wants all students to attain and retain. These big ideas form the foundation for later planning activities that use cognitive taxonomies to differentiate unit and lesson goals and instruction for use with students of varying abilities.

Lesson planning   Once learning targets have been identified, information needed to plan day-to-day activities that will support students to achieve unit outcomes is available. Generally, this preparation leads to lesson plans, which serve as a tool for breaking large units of study into smaller, manageable increments. The amount of time needed for a particular lesson will vary according to the complexity of the learning targets and the number of tasks needed to scaffold students' readiness levels to meet those targets. Generally, lesson plans set forth the topic or theme of the lesson, clear expectations as to the purpose of the lesson (rationale), how the lesson will be conducted (activities), what students are expected to accomplish (objective), and how those accomplishments will be measured and accounted (evaluation).

Importantly to the success of students with significant cognitive disabilities, the lesson plan should also describe the cognitive, affective, and communicative and physical/health demands required of each learning target, and identify where various students will enter the learning sequence and what each student will need to succeed. Janney and Snell (2004) have forwarded the need for teachers to design lessons in which objectives with varying degrees of difficulty have been identified for students with differing learning needs and abilities, a process referred to as multilevel curriculum. Within the lesson planning process, teachers can create objectives that vary across learning abilities but which address the same overall lesson goal by using cognitive or learning taxonomies. Cognitive taxonomies are used to classify the cognitive demands of learning targets. Perhaps the most familiar cognitive taxonomy is the one developed by Bloom, Englehart, Furst, Hill, and Krathwohl (1956). Bloom's taxonomy is a means of categorizing the cognitive skills students use when achieving learning targets. As one ascends Bloom's taxonomy, the cognitive demands from students are more complex.

As cognitive taxonomies are applied in lesson planning activities, teachers track whether they are introducing students to increasingly complex skills and content. When learning objectives are set, students are expected to demonstrate their competence across levels of higher-ordered thinking skills and content types. Teachers should not automatically assume that students with significant cognitive disabilities can perform only at lower levels of cognitive taxonomies. Instead, they should apply what they understand about a student's cognitive abilities and create materials and supports that allow them to achieve at multiple levels.

Trends, Issues, and Future Directions

The IDEA access to the general education curriculum mandates were intended to improve educational outcomes for all students with disability by aligning special educational practices with school reform initiatives. Such desired outcomes involve increased participation and progress in the general curriculum. There is not universal agreement in the field with regard to the extent to which students with significant cognitive disabilities should be engaged in standards-based learning in core content areas. There is general agreement, however, that holding students with significant cognitive disabilities to higher expectations is a worthwhile endeavor and, as highlighted in this chapter, there is emerging evidence that students with significant cognitive disabilities can benefit from instruction in core content areas.

This chapter has outlined actions to achieve this outcome that focus on all levels of the educational process, beginning with standards setting and curriculum design, and involving the district, school, and classroom level actions detailed in this chapter, students with significant cognitive disabilities can receive an educational program that is based both on the general curriculum and the student's unique learning needs. Key elements that will determine the answer to the question as to whether students with significant cognitive disabilities can benefit from instruction in core content areas are in their early phases of development and lack the empirical support that would validate their inclusion in educational programs for students with severe disabilities. We know far too little about the impact of UDL principals on educational outcomes for students with severe disabilities. Likewise, while there exists a robust evidence-base for various curriculum adaptations to enable students with high incidence disabilities to learn curriculum content, most of these strategies have not been modified and/or evaluated for use with students with severe disabilities. There is a substantial literature base that supports the use of student-directed learning strategies with students with severe disabilities, but limited research regarding the impact of this or any other instructional strategy on actual progress in the general education curriculum.

It's important, as well, to emphasize that the intent of IDEA was not to eliminate a focus on functional or life skills instruction for students with significant cognitive disabilities, but to add to the equation the opportunity for students with severe disabilities to learn the same curriculum that is deemed important for all students. We certainly need to know how to more effectively achieve these outcomes while still preparing students for important life outcomes. Nevertheless, given findings that alternate assessment and alternate achievement standards developed for use with students with significant cognitive disabilities have, to this point, more in common with functional content than academic content, there is also reason to be concerned that the intent of IDEA to raise expectations for all students is being watered down for students with significant cognitive disabilities. Finally, there is a need for teacher training and personnel preparation models that prepare all educators, both special and general educators, to implement high quality instructional strategies and to modify and adapt the curriculum to support students with significant cognitive disabilities.

Discussion Questions

These questions can be used as a basis for online discussion forums or as a starting point for discussion in the college classroom.

1. Do you feel that students with more significant disabilities should be included in the general education classroom? Why or why not?

2. Do you feel you are equipped as a classroom teacher to meet the needs of students with significant disabilities in the general education classroom? Why or why not?

3. Do you feel the students with significant disabilities have access to the general education classroom and curriculum in your school building? Describe how this occurs in your experience.

4. Do you feel the students with significant disabilities need access to the general education classroom and curriculum in your school building? Why do you feel this way?

References

Agran, M., Alper, S., & Wehmeyer, M. (2002). Access to the general curriculum for students with significant disabilities: What it means to teachers. *Education and Training in Mental Retardation and Developmental Disabilities, 37,* 123–133.

Agran, M., Blanchard, C. Hughes, C., & Wehmeyer, M. L. (2002). Increasing the problem-solving skills of students with severe disabilities participating in general education. *Remedial and Special Education, 23,* 279–288.

Agran, M., King-Sears, M. E., Wehmeyer, M. L., & Copeland, S. R. (2003). *Student-directed learning.* Baltimore: Paul H. Brookes.

Agran, M., Sinclair, T., Alper, S., Cavin, M., Wehmeyer, M., & Hughes, C. (2005). Using self-monitoring to increase following-direction skills of students with moderate to severe disabilities in general education. *Education and Training in Developmental Disabilities, 40,* 3–13.

Agran, M., Wehmeyer, M., Cavin, M., & Palmer, S. (in press). Promoting engagement in the general education classroom and access to the general education curriculum for students with cognitive disabilities. *Education and Training in Developmental Disabilities.*

Barger-Anderson, R., Isherwood, R., & Merhaut, J. (2010, February). *The Co-Design Model: A collaborative approach to inclusive education.* Paper presented at the 47th Annual International Conference of the Learning Disabilities Association of America, Baltimore, MD.

Bearne, E. (Ed.). (1996). *Differentiation and diversity in the primary school.* New York: Routledge.

Blalock, G. (1991). Paraprofessionals: Critical team members in our special education programs. *Intervention in School and Clinic, 26*(4), 200–214.

Bloom, B. S., Englehart, M. B., Furst, E. J., Hill, W. H., & Krathwohl, D. R. (1956.). *Taxonomy of educational objectives. The classification of educational goals. Handbook I: Cognitive domain.* New York: McKay.

Browder, D. M., Ahlgrim-Delzell, L., Courtade, G., Gibbs, S. L., & Flowers, C. (2008). Evaluation of the effectiveness of an early literacy program for students with significant developmental disabilities. *Exceptional Children, 75*(1), 33–52.

Browder, D., Flowers, C., Ahlgrim-Delzell, L., Karvonen, M., Spooner, F. & Algozzine, R. (2004). The alignment of alternate assessment content with academic and functional curricula. *The Journal of Special Education, 37*(4), 211–223.

Browder, D. M., Mims, P. J., Spooner, F., Ahgrim-Delzell, L., & Lee, A. (2008). Teaching elementary students with multiple disabilities to participate in shared stories. *Research and Practice for Persons with Severe Disabilities, 33*(1-2), 3–12.

Browder, D., & Spooner, F. (2006). *Teaching language arts, math, and science to students with significant cognitive disabilities.* Baltimore: Paul H. Brookes.

Browder, D. M., Spooner, F., Wakeman, S., Trela, K., & Baker, J. N. (2006). Aligning instruction with academic content standards: Finding the link. *Research and Practice for Persons with Severe Disabilities, 31*(4), 309–321.

Browder, D. M., Trela, K., & Jimenez, B. (2007). Training teachers to follow a task analysis to engage middle school students with moderate and severe developmental disabilities in grade-appropriate literature. *Focus on Autism and Other Developmental Disabilities, 22*(4), 206–219.

Browder, D. M., Wakeman, S. Y., & Flowers, C. (2006). Assessment of progress in the general curriculum for students with disabilities. *Theory into Practice, 45*(3), 249–259.

Bryant, D. P., Smith, D. D., & Bryant, B. R. (2008). *Teaching students with special needs in inclusive classrooms.* Boston, MA: Allyn & Bacon.

Buswell, B., Schaffner, C., & Seyler, A. (1999). *Opening doors: Connecting students to curriculum, classmates, and learning.* Colorado Springs: PEAK Parent Center, Inc.

Butler, F. M., Miller, S. P., Lee, K., & Pierce, T. (2001). Teaching mathematics to students with mild-to-moderate mental retardation: A review of the literature. *Mental Retardation, 39*(1), 20–31.

California Department of Education (2015, July). Definition of MTSS. Retrieved from http://www.cde.ca.gov/ci/cr/ri/mtsscomprti2.asp.

Carter, E. W., Cushing, L. S., Clark, N. M., & Kennedy, C. H. (2005). Effects of peer support interventions on students' access to the general curriculum and social interactions. *Research and Practice for Persons with Severe Disabilities, 30*(1), 15–25.

Carter, E. W., & Kennedy, C. H. (2006). Promoting access to the general curriculum using peer support strategies. *Research and Practice for Persons with Severe Disabilities, 31*(4), 284–292.

Carter, E. W., Sisco, L. G., Melekoglu, M. A., & Kurkowski, C. (2007). Peer supports as an alternative to individually assigned paraprofessionals in inclusive high school classrooms. *Research and Practice for Persons with Severe Disabilities, 32*(4), 213–227.

Center for Applied Special Technology (CAST). (1998–1999). The national center on accessing the general curriculum, http://www.cast. org/initiatives/nationalcenter.html.

Clark, N. M., Cushing, L.S., & Kennedy, C. H. (2004). An intensive onsite technical assistance model to promote inclusive educational practices for students with disabilities in middle school and high school. *Research and Practice for Persons with Severe Disabilities, 29*(4), 253–262.

Cole, C. M., Waldron, N., & Majd, M. (2004). Academic progress of students across inclusive and traditional settings. *Mental Retardation, 42*(2), 136–144.

Collins, B. C., Evans, A., Creech-Galloway, C., Karl, J., & Miller, A. (2007). Comparison of the acquisition and maintenance of teaching functional and core content sight words in special and general education settings. *Focus on Autism and Other Developmental Disabilities, 22*(4), 220–233.

Conner, C. M., & Morrison, F. J. (2014). Services or Programs that Influence Young Children's Academic Success and School Completion. Encyclopedia of Early Childhood Development, 2, 1–10.

Cook, L., & Friend, M. (1996). Co-teaching: Guidelines for creating effective practices. *Focus on Exceptional Children, 28,* 1–16.

Costa, A. L. & Kallick, B. (2008) *Learning and leading with habits of mind: 16 essential characteristics for success.* Alexandria, VA: ASCD.

Costa, A. L. & Kallick, B. (2009) *Habits of mind across the curriculum: Practical and creative strategies for teachers.* Alexandria, VA: ASCD.

Courtade, G. R., Spooner, F., & Browder, D. M. (2006). Review of studies with students with significant cognitive disabilities which link to science standards. *Research and Practice for Persons with Severe Disabilities, 32*(1), 43–49.

Csikszentmihalyi, M. (1997). *Finding Flow: The Psychology of Engagement with Everyday Life.* New York: Basic Books.

Danielson, C. (1996). *Enhancing Professional Practice: A Framework for Teaching.* Alexandria, VA: Association for Supervision and Curriculum Development. ED 403 245.

Dymond, S. K., Renzaglia, A., Gilson, C. L., & Slagor, M. T. (2007). Defining access to the general curriculum for high school students with significant cognitive disabilities. *Research and Practice for Persons with Severe Disabilities, 32*(1), 1–15.

Dymond, S. K., Renzaglia, A., Rosenstein, A., Chun, E. J., Banks, R. A., Niswander, V., & Gilson, C. L. (2006). Using a participatory action research approach to create a universally designed inclusive high school Science course; A case study. *Research and Practice for Persons with Severe Disabilities, 31*(4), 293–308.

Federal Register. (1999, March 12). Washington, DC: U.S. Government Printing Office.

Friend, M. (2005). *The power of 2* (2nd ed.). Port Chester, NY: National Professional Resources.

Friend, M. (2007). *Co-teaching defined.* Retrieved from http://www.marilynfriend.com/basics. htm

Friend, M. (2011). *Special education: Contemporary perspectives for school professionals* (3rd ed.). Boston, MA: Pearson.

Fuchs, L.S., Powell, S. R., Seethaler, P. M., Cirino, P. T., Fletcher, J. M., Fuchs, D., Hamlett, C. L., & Zumeta, R.O. (2009). Remediating number combination and word problem deficits among students with mathematics difficulties: A randomized control trial. *Journal of Educational Psychology*, 101, 561–576.

Gately, S. E., & Gately, F. J. (2001). Understanding co-teaching components. *Teaching Exceptional Children, 33*, 40–47.

Gregory, G. (2005) *Differentiating instruction with style.* Thousand Oaks, CA: Corwin Press.

Hasbrouck, J. E., Ihnot, C., & Rogers, G. (1999). "Read Naturally": A strategy to increase oral reading fluency. *Reading Research and Instruction*, 39(1), 27–38.

Hasbrouck, J. E., & Tindal, G. (1991). Curriculum-based oral reading fluency norms for students in grades 2 through 5. *Teaching Exceptional Children*, 24(3), 41–44.

Howell, R., Patton, S., & Deiotte, M. (2008). *Understanding response to intervention: A practical guide to systemic implementation.* Bloomington, IN: Solution Tree Press.

Hoyt-Goldsmith, D. (1998). *Celebrating Chinese new year.* New York, NY: Holiday House. Individuals with Disabilities Education Improvement Act (IDEA) of 2004, PL 108–146, 20 U.S.C. §§ 1400 *et seq.*

Hughes, C., Copeland, S. R., Agran, M., Wehmeyer, M. L., Rodi, M. S., & Presley, J. A. (2002). Using self-monitoring to improve performance in general education high school classes. *Education and Training in Mental Retardation and Developmental Disabilities, 37*, 262–271.

Individuals with Disabilites Act (IDEA) of 2004, P. L. 108–446, 108th Congress (2004).

Isherwood, R. S., & Barger-Anderson, R. (2007). Factors affecting the adoption of co-teaching models in inclusive classrooms: One school's journey from mainstreaming to inclusion. *Journal of Ethnographic and Qualitative Research, 2,* 121–128.

Janney, R., & Snell, M. (2004). *Modifying schoolwork: Teachers' guides to inclusive practices* (2nd ed.). Baltimore: Paul H. Brookes.

Jimenez, B. A., Browder, D. M., & Courtade, G. R. (2008). Teaching an algebraic equation to high school students with moderate developmental disabilities. *Education and Training in Developmental Disabilities, 43*(2), 266–274.

Jorgensen, C. M., McSheehan, M., & Sonnenmeier, R. M. (2010). *The Beyond Access Model: Promoting membership, participation, and learning for students with disabilities in the general education classroom.* Baltimore: Paul H. Brookes.

Jung, C. G. (1923) *Psychological types.* Trans. H.G. Baynes. New York: Harcourt, Brace & Company.

Karvonen, M. & Huynh, H. (2007). Relationship between IEP characteristics and test scores on an alternate assessment for students with significant cognitive disabilities. *Applied Measurement in Education, 20*(3), 273–300.

Kiernan, L. (Producer). (1997). *Differentiating instruction* [A video staff development set]. Alexandria, VA: Association for Supervision and Curriculum Development.

Kise, J. A. G. (2007) *Differentiation through personality types: A framework for instruction, assessment, and classroom management.* Thousand Oaks, CA: Corwin Press.

Konrad, M., Trela, K., & Test, D. W. (2006). Using IEP goals and objectives to teach paragraph writing to high school students with physical and cognitive disabilities. *Education and Training in Developmental Disabilities, 41*(2), 111–124.

Kortering, L. J., McLannon, T. W., & Braziel, P. M. (2008). Universal Design for Learning: A look at what algebra and biology students with and without high incidence conditions are saying. *Remedial and Special Education, 29*(6), 352–363.

Lee, S. H., Wehmeyer, M. L., Palmer, S. B., Soukup, J. H., & Little, T. D. (2008). Self-determination and access to the general education curriculum. *The Journal of Special Education, 42,* 91–107.

Lee, S. H., Wehmeyer, M. L., Soukup, J. H., & Palmer, S. B. (2010). Impact of curriculum modifications on access to the general education curriculum for students with disabilities. *Exceptional Children, 76*(2), 213–233.

Madea, B. (1994). *The multiage classroom: An inside look at one community of learners.* Cypress, CA: Creative Teaching Press.

Matzen, K., Ryndak, D., & Nakao, T. (in press). Middle school teams increasing access to general education for students with significant disabilities: Issues encountered and activities observed across contexts. *Remedial and Special Education.*

Mamchur, C. (1996) *A teacher's guide to cognitive type theory and learning style.* Alexandria, VA: ASCD.

McCarthy, B. (1982) *The 4mat system.* Arlington Heights, IL: Excel Publishing.

McSheehan, M., Sonnenmeier, R. M., Jorgensen, C. M., & Turner, K. (2006). Beyond communication access: Promoting learning of the general education curriculum by students with significant disabilities. *Topics in Language Disorders, 26*(3), 266–290.

Murawski, W. W., & Dieker, L. A. (2004). Tips and strategies for co-teaching at the secondary level. *Teaching Exceptional Children, 36,* 52–58.

Myers, I. B. (1962/1998) *The Myers-Briggs Type Indicator.* Palo Alto, CA: Consulting Psychologists Press.

Nolet, V., & McLaughlin, M. (2000). *Accessing the general curriculum.* Thousand Oaks, CA; Corwin Press.

No Child Left Behind Act of 2001, PL 107-110, 115 Stat. 1425, 20 U.S.C. §§ 6301 *et seq.*

Orkwis, R., & McLane, K. (1998, Fall). A curriculum every student can use: Design principles for student access. *ERIC/OSEP Topical Brief.* Reston, VA: Council for Exceptional Children.

Pajak, E. (2003) *Honoring diverse teaching styles: A guide for supervisors.* Alexandria, VA: ASCD.

Palmer, S. B., Wehmeyer, M. L., Gipson, K., & Agran, M. (2004). Promoting access to the general curriculum by teaching self-determination skills. *Exceptional Children, 70,* 427–439.

Payne, D. & Van Sant, S. (2009) *Great minds don't think alike: Success for students through the application of psychological type in schools.* Gainsville, FL: Center for Applications of Psychological Type.

Rice, D., & Zigmond, N. (2000). Co-teaching in secondary schools: Teacher reports of developments in Australian and American classrooms. *Learning Disabilities Research and Practice, 15*(4), 190–197.

Riggs, C. G. (2005). To teachers: What paraeducators want you to know. *Teaching Exceptional Children, 36*(5), 8–12.

Roach, A. T., & Elliott, S. N. (2006). The influence of access to general education curriculum on alternate assessment performance of students with significant cognitive disabilities. *Educational Evaluation and Policy Analysis, 28*(2), 181–194.

Silver, H. F., & Strong, R. W. (2004). *Learning style inventory for students.* Ho-Ho-Kus, NJ: Thoughtful Education Press.

Silver, H. F., & Strong, R. W. (2010). *Learning style inventory for students* (online edition). Ho-Ho-Kus, NJ: Thoughtful Education Press.

Silver, H. F., Strong, R. W., & Perini, M. J. (2000). *So each may learn: Integrating learning styles and multiple intelligences.* Alexandria, VA: ASCD.

Sonnenmeir, R. M., McSheehan, M., & Jorgensen, C. M. (2005). A case study of team supports for a student with autism's communication and engagement within the general education curriculum: Preliminary report of the Beyond Access Model. *Augmentative and Alternative Communication, 21*(2), 101–115.

Soukup, J. H., Wehmeyer, M. L., Bashinski, S. M., & Bovaird, J. (2007). Classroom variables and access to the general education curriculum of students with intellectual and developmental disabilities. *Exceptional Children, 74,* 101–120.

Spooner, F., Baker, J. N., Harris, A. A., Ahlgrim-Delzell, & Browder, D. M. (2007). Effects of training in Universal Design for Learning on lesson plan development. *Remedial and Special Education, 28*(2), 108–116.

Spooner, F., Dymond, S. K., Smith, A., & Kennedy, C. H. (2006). What we know and need to know about accessing the general curriculum for students with significant cognitive disabilities. *Research and Practice for Persons with Severe Disabilities, 31*(4), 277–283.

Stainback, W., Stainback, S., Stefanich, G., & Alper, S. (1996). Learning in inclusive classrooms: What about the curriculum? In S. Stainback & W. Stainback (Eds.), *Inclusion: A guide for educators* (pp. 209–219). Baltimore: Paul H. Brookes.

Sternberg, R. J., Torff, B., & Grigorenko, E. L. (1998). Teaching triarchically improves student achievement. *Journal of Educational Psychology*, 90(3), 374–384. EJ 576 492.

Tomlinson, C.A. (1995). *How to Differentiate Instruction in Mixed-Ability Classrooms.* Alexandria, VA: Association for Supervision and Curriculum Development. ED 386 301.

Tomlinson, C.A. (1996). *Differentiating instruction for mixed-ability classrooms* [A professional inquiry kit]. Alexandria, VA: Association for Supervision and Curriculum Development.

Tomlinson, C.A. (1999). *The Differentiated Classroom: Responding to the Needs of All Learners.* Alexandria, VA: Association for Supervision and Curriculum Development. ED 429 944.

Tomlinson, C. A. (August, 2000). Differentiation of Instruction in the Elementary Grades. ERIC Digest. ERIC Clearinghouse on Elementary and Early Childhood Education.

U.S. Department of Education, Institute of Education Sciences, What Works Clearinghouse. (2013, July). *Beginning Reading intervention report: Read Naturally®.* Retrieved from http://whatworks.ed.gov.

U.S. Department of Education (1995). *Testimony of Richard Riley, Secretary, U.S. Department of Education: Hearings before the Committee on Economic and Educational Opportunities*

Subcommittee on Early Childhood, Youth and Families, House of Representatives, 104th Cong. Retrieved from http://www.ed.gov/Speeches/06-1995/idea-1.html.

U.S. Department of Education (2003). *Title I-Improving the academic achievement of the disadvantaged*: Proposed Rule, 68 Fe. Reg. 13, 797–798.

U.S. Department of Education (2005). Alternate achievement standards for students with the most significant cognitive disabilities: Non-regulatory guidance. Washington, DC: Author. Retrieved October 4, 2009, from http://74.125.95.132/search?q=cache:W12oht6GHgYJ:www.ed.gov/policy/elsec/guid/altguidance.pdf+students+with+the+most+significant+cognitive+disabilities&cd=1&hl=en&ct=clnk&gl=us.

Villa, R. A., Thousand, J. S., & Nevin, A. I. (2004). *A guide to co-teaching: Practical tips for facilitating student learning.* Thousand Oaks, CA: Sage Publications.

Vygotsky, L. (1986). *Thought and Language.* Cambridge, MA: MIT Press.

Wehmeyer, M. L., Field, S., Doren, B., Jones, B., & Mason, C. (2004). Self-determination and student involvement in standards-based reform. *Exceptional Children, 70*, 413–425.

Wehmeyer, M. L., Hughes, C., Agran, M., Garner. N., & Yeager, D. (2003). Student-directed learning strategies to promote the progress of students with intellectual disability in inclusive classrooms. *International Journal of Inclusive Education, 7*, 415–428.

Wehmeyer, M. L., Lance, G. D., & Bashinski, S. (2002). Promoting access to the general curriculum for students with mental retardation: A multi-level model. *Education and Training in Mental Retardation and Developmental Disabilities, 37*, 223–234.

Wehmeyer, M. L., Lattin, D., Lapp-Rincker, G., & Agran, M. (2003). Access to the general curriculum of middle-school students with mental retardation: An observational study. *Remedial and Special Education, 24*, 262–272.

Wehmeyer, M. L., Palmer, S., Agran, M., Mithaug, D., & Martin, J. (2000). Promoting causal agency: The Self-Determined Learning Model of Instruction. *Exceptional Children, 66*, 439–453.

Wehmeyer, M. L., Sands, D. J., Knowlton, H. E., & Kozleski, E. B. (2002). *Teaching students with mental retardation: Providing access to the general curriculum.* Baltimore: Paul H. Brookes.

Werts, M. G., Culatta, R. A., & Tompkins, J. R. (2007). *Fundamentals of special education. What every teacher needs to know* (3rd ed.). Upper Saddle River, NJ: Pearson.

Whitfield, S. (1998). *Animals of the Chinese zodiac.* Northampton, MA: Interlink.

Winebrenner, S. (1992). *Teaching Gifted Kids in the Regular Classroom.* Minneapolis, MN: Free Spirit.

Winebrenner, S. (1996). *Teaching Kids with Learning Difficulties in the Regular Classroom.* Minneapolis, MN: Free Spirit. ED 396 502.

Ysseldyke, J., Dennison, A., & Nelson, R. (2003). *Large-scale assessment and accountability systems: Positive consequences for students with disabilities* (Synthesis Report 51). Minneapolis: University of Minnesota, National Center on Educational Outcomes. Retrieved December 8, 2009, from http://education.umn.edu/NCEO/OnlinePubs/Synthesis51.html.

Zigmond, N., & Magiera, K. (2001). A focus on co-teaching (use caution). *Current Practice Alerts from the Division for Learning Disabilities and Division for Research of the Council for Exceptional Children, 6,* 1–4. Retrieved from the "Use Caution" section of http://www.dldcec.org/alerts/.

CPSIA information can be obtained
at www.ICGtesting.com
Printed in the USA
LVHW012338160721
692906LV00004B/24